SUBVERTING GREED

Religious Perspectives
on the Global Economy

FAITH MEETS FAITH

An Orbis Series in Interreligious Dialogue

Paul F. Knitter and William R. Burrows, General Editors

In the contemporary world, the many religions and spiritualities stand in need of greater communication and cooperation. More than ever before, they must speak to, learn from, and work with each other in order to maintain their vital identities and to contribute to fashioning a better world.

The FAITH MEETS FAITH Series seeks to promote interreligious dialogue by providing an open forum for exchange among followers of different religious paths. While the Series wants to encourage creative and bold responses to questions arising from contemporary appreciations of religious plurality, it also recognizes the multiplicity of basic perspectives concerning the methods and content of interreligious dialogue.

Although rooted in a Christian theological perspective, the Series does not limit itself to endorsing any single school of thought or approach. By making available to both the scholarly community and the general public works that represent a variety of religious and methodological viewpoints, FAITH MEETS FAITH seeks to foster an encounter among followers of the religions of the world on matters of common concern.

FAITH MEETS FAITH SERIES

SUBVERTING GREED

Religious Perspectives on the Global Economy

Edited by

PAUL F. KNITTER

and

CHANDRA MUZAFFAR

ORBIS BOOKS
Maryknoll, New York

published in association with
Boston Research Center for the 21st Century

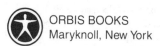

Eighth Printing, May 2008

Founded in 1970, Orbis Books endeavors to publish works that enlighten the mind, nourish the spirit, and challenge the conscience. The publishing arm of the Maryknoll Fathers and Brothers, Orbis seeks to explore the global dimensions of the Christian faith and mission, to invite dialogue with diverse cultures and religious traditions, and to serve the cause of reconciliation and peace. The books published reflect the opinions of their authors and are not meant to represent the official position of the Maryknoll Society. To obtain more information about Maryknoll and Orbis Books, please visit our website at www.maryknoll.org.

The Boston Research Center for the 21st Century (BRC) is an international peace institute founded in 1993 by Daisaku Ikeda, a Buddhist peace activist and president of Soka Gakkai International, an association of Buddhist organizations in 181 countries. The BRC brings together scholars and activists in dialogue on common values across cultures and religions, seeking in this way to support an evolving global ethic for a peaceful twenty-first century. Human rights, nonviolence, environmental ethics, economic justice, education for global citizenship, and women's leadership for peace are focal points of the Center's work. The Center is located at 396 Harvard Street, Cambridge, MA 02138. Tel: 617-491-1090; Fax: 617-491-1169; E-mail: center@brc21.org; website: www.brc21.org.

Project Manager, Patti M. Marxsen. Style and copy-editing, Helen Marie Casey.

Published by Orbis Books, Maryknoll, NY 10545-0308 in association with Boston Research Center for the 21st Century.

Manufactured in the United States of America.

Library of Congress Cataloging in Publication Data

Subverting greed : religious perspectives on the global economy / edited by Paul F. Knitter and Chandra Muzaffar.
p. cm. — (Faith meets faith)
Includes bibliographical references and index.
ISBN 1-57075-446-2
1. Globalization—Moral and ethical aspects. 2. Globalization—Religious aspects. 3. International economic relations—Moral and ethical aspects. 4. International economic relations—Religious aspects. 5. Business ethics. 6. Economics—Moral and ethical aspects. 7. Economics—Religious aspects. I. Knitter, Paul F. II. Chandra Muzaffar, 1947- III. Series.
HF1359 .S8665 2002
174'.4—dc21

2002005460

In Memory of

Vittorio D. Falsina

1962 – 2001

CONTENTS

PREFACE

This book is dedicated to Vittorio Falsina, who devoted his life to the same goal that has inspired our effort. When my colleagues and I at the Boston Research Center first met Vittorio, he was engaged in an ambitious project at Harvard University's Center for the Study of World Religions. That project, "Recasting Globalization: Religion, Culture and Ethnicity," was Vittorio's passion and lives on, even after his death in August 2001. As Vittorio explained in a guest interview in the BRC's spring 2001 newsletter, through his work on this project, he hoped to provide "an ethical compass to reorient the process of globalization toward a more human, sustainable, peaceful globalization."

With *Subverting Greed*, we, too, seek to provide an ethical compass based on multireligious insights that will stimulate dialogue, particularly in college classrooms. In these settings, *Subverting Greed* can act as a counterweight to traditional economic texts that are sometimes blind to the human dimension hidden beneath theories and formulas. If even one future leader finds encouragement in these pages to imagine and then work for that entirely possible world in which absolute poverty no longer exists, then our efforts will have been worthwhile.

At a time when religion in its fanatical, dangerously closed form has enabled acts of terrible destruction, interfaith partnerships among religious believers working for a better world are more important than ever. One such partnership gave birth to this book. Paul Knitter, a Christian theologian, and Chandra Muzaffar, a Muslim scholar, came together with our Buddhist-inspired peace institute to create *Subverting Greed.* When the two editors first met at Gethsemani Abbey in the summer of 2000 to plan the book, the title took shape from an insight they shared—that all the world's religions can agree on at least one thing in regard to economic matters: *Greed is not an admirable human trait.*

The editors' original insight has been borne out by essays from the distinguished array of scholar-practitioners who accepted our invitation to contribute to this book. In separate chapters as wide-ranging as they are cohesive, these contributors ably respond to a common set of questions in regard to their religious traditions and the relationship between their traditions and the world. Each essay touches on one religious tradition's critique of the present economic order, its understanding of economic theory, its economic record (just and unjust), and its potential for making distinctive contributions to global economic justice.

Publishers, knowing the difficulties of shaping a multi-author work into a coherent whole, think twice before accepting such projects. That's where BRC project manager Patti M. Marxsen comes into the picture. Without Patti's skilled and steady hand guiding each essay to completion, her communication with authors and editors on five continents, her unfailing tact, timing, and style, this book would still be a back-burner item on a publisher's wish list. We are grateful to Orbis Books and the managing editor, Bill Burrows, for their faith in us, and especially in Patti, as we pulled numerous rabbits out of the hat, one by one. And last but not least, our appreciation goes to Helen Marie Casey, writer-editor *extraordinaire*, who came to our aid as freelance copyeditor and tiebreaker on style decisions big and small.

—Virginia Straus
Executive Director
Boston Research Center for the 21st Century

FOREWORD

Thirty years ago, the Club of Rome sounded the warning in *The Limits to Growth* that the pursuit of growth and prosperity driven by unrestrained greed was beckoning the destruction of humankind. I subsequently held a series of dialogues with the Club of Rome founder, Aurelio Peccei, which were published in English as *Before It Is Too Late*. I will never forget the dire prognostication of the future of human civilization that Dr. Peccei expressed—"man," he said, "has never been so much in danger as he is now, at the peak of his power." Today, at the start of the twenty-first century, the circumstances that so concerned Dr. Peccei have become ever more pronounced.

The Limits to Growth addressed the issue of earth's dwindling natural resources and energy reserves. Now, in addition, the rapid advance of globalization has magnified the problems of poverty and economic inequality and has brought to all corners of earth such crises as the destruction of the natural environment and the collapse of traditional cultures.

The Boston Research Center for the 21st Century (BRC) was founded to promote and support the quest for solutions to problems such as these. This volume, *Subverting Greed: Religious Perspectives on the Global Economy*, is being published in the Orbis Faith Meets Faith Series as part of the Center's endeavors to further the cause of economic justice. It examines the role of the world's religious traditions in finding ways to conquer human greed and transform the global economy, which all too often leads to the victimization and exploitation of the vulnerable. *Subverting Greed* is designed to seek out and bring together the wisdom that world religions are able to offer.

It is impossible not to be deeply pained by the fact that at present substantially more than a billion people—one member in five of our human family—are living in abject poverty. The United Nations Development Program (UNDP), which has been working to ameliorate this situation, has warned: "if present trends continue, the global economy will be gargantuan in its excesses and grotesque in its inequalities." But the problem is not one that operates in the political and economic dimensions alone. It strikes at the way all contemporary humans live their lives and at our most profound impulses and motivations. Systemic reforms and the promotion of international cooperation must be pursued urgently. But unless these are reinforced by a willingness to re-examine our attitude to human life itself, they will, I fear, remain incomplete.

Buddhism speaks of deluded impulses—greed, anger, and fundamental ignorance—as the three poisons. It understands these elements as underlying and further compounding the chaotic crises that beset human society. Of these three poisons, Buddhism teaches that greed constitutes a negative energy that blinds us to the existence of others as we engage ourselves in an open-ended and finally fruitless search for gratification.

The words of the Bengali poet-sage Rabindranath Tagore precisely sum up this aspect of the human psyche: "Avarice is an evil passion, and for that reason it cannot create. Man's spiritual nexus is weakened when avarice becomes the motive power of a civilization. The greater the material wealth, strength, and prosperity conferred by such a civilization, the less potent is the spiritual power of man." The eradication of desire, however, is a practical impossibility. Indeed, totally denying desire would deprive us of that life energy that is essential to our existence as human beings.

Wherein lies the solution?

I believe that the mastery of desire, which lies at the heart of all religious ethics, is essential. Specifically, I believe it is a question of how to transform and redirect the energy of human desire away from indulgence and destruction, and toward revitalization and growth.

The Buddhist teacher Nichiren, who was active in thirteenth-century Japan, explained this point based on the understanding of desire taught by Mahayana Buddhism—"We burn the firewood of earthly desires and behold the fire of enlightened wisdom before our eyes."

This describes the qualitative transformation of the "energy of earthly desires"—deluded impulses such as the three poisons—into the "energy of Buddhahood," which is resplendent with compassion and wisdom. In essence, the purpose of living in an ethical and moral way is for human beings to free themselves from the thrall of greed and the other poisons and to transform these poisons into positive value by redirecting negative energy in a positive, creative direction.

All the great religious traditions contain their own systems of ethics that address fundamental human concerns. For example, injunctions against killing and stealing respectively teach nonviolence through the conquest of hatred and the realization of economic justice through the conquest of greed. In other words, they go further than just prohibiting direct theft or exploitation but more largely indicate that we should follow the path of interdependence and creative coexistence with the whole of humankind seeking the shared prosperity of humanity and a mutual flourishing with the natural world.

In the *Brahma Net Sutra,* one of the Mahayana teachings, we find the passage: "A bodhisattva must always evoke from the Buddha nature compassion and devotion to help any and every kind of person, to bring about good fortune, and to provide comfort." In short, this calls upon us "to do as we would be done by"—never to build our own happiness on the unhappiness of others. This is one of the core ethical postulates of Buddhism.

In our contemporary world, as the powerful forces of the global economy daily exacerbate the crises of global injustice and poverty, all individuals and communities involved in economic activity are called upon with increasing insistence to rise above the cold logic of the market and, instead, to demonstrate new models of genuinely creative coexistence informed by a robust ethical perspective.

The world's great religious traditions can certainly contribute to enhancing the fundamental human ethics that must underlie all economic activities if they are to generate healthy and sustainable development. "Vitality," according to Paul Tillich, one of the twentieth century's most important religious scholars, "is the power of creating beyond oneself without losing oneself."

In recent years, as more and more people rethink their attitudes toward a global economic system exclusively devoted to quantitative expansion and growth, human development has become an increasingly key concept. Genuine human development can, I believe, become a reality to the extent that it is based on a trust directed toward the vitality inherent in human life.

Within this vitality the qualities of wisdom, love, purpose, tolerance, and mutual respect are contained and manifest themselves as fairness, justice, freedom, and creative coexistence. The mission of religion is to actualize the potentials within this natural vitality, to tap the wellspring of humanity's intrinsic spirituality.

Further, all great religious traditions have the responsibility to show us how, through self-control, we may lead the kind of moral lives that make us truly human, and how we may establish an ethical basis for all human endeavors, including the rapidly globalizing fields of economics, politics, knowledge, and information technology.

In this sense, I am deeply convinced that this collection of essays by scholars representing the world's great religions, the second in the series that began with *Subverting Hatred: The Challenge of Nonviolence in Religious Traditions*, will surely contribute to a global society in which all people may equally enjoy happiness.

Finally, I extend my heartfelt gratitude to all who have worked to make this publication possible, especially the joint editors, Dr. Paul F. Knitter and Dr. Chandra Muzaffar.

—Daisaku Ikeda
Founder, Boston Research Center for the 21st Century
President, Soka Gakkai International

Introduction

By Paul F. Knitter

This was an opportunity we could not afford to let slip by. That, essentially, was the way Dr. Chandra Muzaffar and I responded to the invitation from the Boston Research Center to edit this book. Even though our plates were full, we knew we just had to find room for this project because we felt the urgent need to bring the global reality of "the market" and the global reality of "the religions" into conversation. These ever-present realities are two global powers that, for too long, have neglected each other, and this book offered an opportunity to do something about that.

On the one hand, the increasingly globalized market is producing unprecedented wealth and an ever-greater disparity between the comfortably rich and the suffering poor. On the other hand, religious communities, each in different ways, warn of the dangers when excessive attachment to "worldly matters" gets in the way of "what really matters." In other words, the economy should matter for the religions, and the captains of the economy might do well to listen to religious leaders and mystics. But first, the world's religious communities must talk more openly with one another about their views on the global economy. Only then could we expect economic leaders to listen attentively. The hope of stimulating such a dialogue is the motivation behind the conception of this book, and it explains why Dr. Muzaffar and I wanted to help.

As we met for the first time with Virginia Straus, executive director of the Boston Research Center (BRC), to clarify our vision for this book, I remembered a parable from the ancient Confucian philosopher Mencius. In order to illustrate what he believed was in the heart of every human being, Mencius proposed the image of a child sitting on the edge of a well. The child loses its balance and is about to fall into the depths of the well. Mencius was convinced that any human being walking past and witnessing the child about to fall would immediately, instinctively, spontaneously reach out to save the child. This is what human beings would *naturally* do, he proposed. Such a natural response illustrates what Mencius called "the mind that cannot bear the sufferings of others."[1] When we meet another human who is suffering and about to fall to his or her death, we *naturally* find ourselves reaching out to help. The suffering of others touches and calls forth something within ourselves, something that defines our humanity.

That, I think, is what is starting to happen within the religious communities of the world. The child perched precariously on the edge of the well, however, has multiplied to become the millions of human beings facing the threat of economic poverty, homelessness, and disease. These people are tottering on the edge of starvation or, worse, watching themselves and their children fall into death or despair. It is this vast population of suffering poor who are currently calling out to the religious communities of the world. More and more, religious persons are noticing, responding, and reaching out as they realize that each of them possesses "the mind that cannot bear the suffering of others."

The essays in this book recognize and record how persons from differing religious beliefs and backgrounds are responding to those among us who are confronting economic despair. At the same time, this book also addresses what is happening to and among the religions when they so respond. Expanding on Mencius's image, we might say that the religions, having reached out, held, and come to know the child, find that the child—in the form of suffering humanity—unexpectedly returns the favor. In short, in responding to the economic plight of the poor, the religions are realizing that the poor are aiding them to better know themselves and to better understand one another. Members of religious groups even find themselves better able to relate to the broader world, including the secular or nonreligious people of the world, as a result of their desire to help. Clearly, reaching out is a gesture that comes full circle as the poor undergo a metamorphosis from the *objects* of religious concern to a *subjective* force that

[1] Mencius 2A: 6.

turns around and helps religions fulfill their own best intentions. In this way, the poor are becoming the mediators who build bridges and new avenues of communication which enable religions to talk among themselves, with the broader academic community, and especially with the world of economists and politicians. With this in mind, I will outline briefly what I mean—and define the goals of this book.

THE POOR AS A CHALLENGE TO OUR VIEW OF THE DIVERSITY OF RELIGIONS

In the academic world, there is a hefty, often heated, discussion about whether the religions of the world really have anything in common. From the perspective of what is called postmodernism, it is argued that in the world of religions, just as in the world of cultures, there are many more differences than there are similarities. This is so because of something we usually do not recognize: that we are always looking at the world—whether it's the world of ants or angels—through our own cultural, historical glasses. We are all *always wearing glasses* as we try to focus on and understand the world around us. And because our glasses are so very different, we are going to see different things or, at least, we are going to see the same thing in very different ways. Therefore, the postmodernists continue, it is unfair for me to pass judgment on you since that would mean that I am judging what you see with your glasses according to what I see with mine. That would be like trying to evaluate the rules of cricket according to the rules of baseball.

This risk of misreading and misjudgment is what the postmodernists are really concerned about when they insist on the dominance of diversity over similarity. For too long, one culture (or one religion)—usually that of the West, whose main religion is Christianity—has been judging other cultures on the basis of its own cultural glasses. More often than not, this approach has led to a view of these other cultures as inferior, primitive, or even "barbaric." As a result, scholars have come up with one of those ten-ton scholarly words to describe the differences between the religions of the world: incommensurable. This simply means that you cannot measure one by the other because they really don't have anything in common; or, if they do, our different cultural glasses prevent the religions from agreeing on what the common ground is.

Certainly, there is value in what the postmodernists are saying and warning of. For too long, the religions, because each was seeing and judging the others through its own glasses, have been burdened by a "better-than-thou" attitude. "God has chosen my religion to be the only true, or the best, religion. And if you can't see that, I just may have to help you see it." And so throughout history, the *encounter* of religions has often become the *clash* of religions. How many wars have been carried out, how much blood has been spilled, because "God is on our side"? With the tragedies of history in mind, we must recognize that the advice of the postmoderns is important: stop judging one religion on the basis of another and abandon the search for a common basis of all religions. Let a thousand religious flowers bloom—each in its own garden!

Yes and no. In trying to promote tolerance and peace among the religions, scholars may be missing opportunities for the religions to cooperate with and learn from one another. The religions, despite their astounding diversity, may have something in common after all. This is what the "child about to fall into the well" seems to be suggesting: If we can't really put our finger on what the religions all have in common within themselves, we can say that the child about to fall into the well is a common concern for many people of all faiths. In other words, if scholars want to argue that there is nothing common *within* the religions, they certainly can't deny that there is something common *surrounding* all of them—the child tottering on the edge of the well, the tremendous suffering among the poor of the planet. In other words, even if the religions don't have a common essence, they can certainly recognize common problems.

And, fortunately, they are all responding to these common problems. People from very diverse religious communities all want to have their say, or make their contribution, in trying to save the child from falling into the well. All of them are trying to do something about the wrenching reality of poverty, hunger, homelessness, and violence. Does this mean that, after all, there is something common to all the religions—"one God" or "one Ultimate"—that is generating this common concern for the sufferings of the poor? That is a philosophical or theological question that we will leave to the theologians and philosophers. Our concern in the pages that follow is to explore how the different religious communities *are* responding to poverty and its causes and then to ask ourselves whether there is anything we can, or must, learn from these various responses.

Because these are important questions, we took great care in assembling the team of contributors to this book. We wanted people who could speak credibly for the different religions, but also people who could speak credibly about the global economy. This meant that we had to find persons with the necessary expertise in economics who also had some established track record in studying the religions, especially their ethical teachings. But even that wasn't enough. We also wanted "experts" who not only could speak knowledgeably about the religions but who could speak from within the religions. In other words, we wanted scholars who were also practitioners trying to live the message and ideals of their particular religious tradition. I trust that readers will find that we managed to line up quite an impressive team.

But since our contributors are mainly scholars of religion, we also wanted to make sure that what they had to say about economics and the global market was based on sound data. In the field of economics, "sound data" are not always readily available, since among professional economists there is such a variety of ways of both determining and analyzing the economy. (Some have claimed that economics is not any more a "hard science" than is theology!) Still, to at least make an effort at a reality check, we had a professional economist with an international perspective read first drafts of all the chapters in this book and provide advice to the authors. Dr. Curtis E. Harvey, professor emeritus of the University of Kentucky and former associate vice-president and director of foreign programs at the American Graduate School of International Management, provided this important service in the creation of this book.

The Poor as Mediators among the Religions

We believe that this book will lead to more dialogue among religious people. As human suffering and the global awareness of it increases, we believe that religious people will want to talk with one another about the need for a religious response to the horrendous sufferings of the poor. In reaching out to the child tottering on the edge of the well, religions will find themselves reaching out to one another. In other words, the poor are becoming mediators among the religions as their suffering calls religious communities to dialogue in search of an effective response.

This is a different kind of dialogue than the interreligious dialogue of the past in which persons from different religions came together to talk about religious matters. They would explain their beliefs to one another, answer one another's questions, and see if there was anything to learn from one another. Or, they might take a more personal or spiritual approach and make use of prayer or meditation as a way to deeper mutual understanding. These were and are all valuable forms of interreligious encounter. But in the kind of dialogue we are describing in this book—the kind that the poor are inviting religious persons to engage in—the starting point is different. The kind of dialogue envisioned in this book takes human and environmental suffering as the primary concern of the conversation. The goal of this dialogue is how to understand and how to stop such suffering. In this new kind of dialogue, therefore, the medium by which religious persons come to know one another is not intellectual or devotional, but ethical. Religious persons worry together about the suffering of the poor, work together in trying to remove such suffering, and wrestle together with all the pains and opposition that inevitably are part of such efforts.

In such an ethical, practical dialogue, participants come to know one another and appreciate one another's traditions in a different way than if they were just talking or praying together. (Again, talking and praying together, of course, have their valuable place.) Their shared concern for the poor, their resolve to relieve the sufferings due to poverty and injustice, their desire to draw on all the resources that religion may offer to correct the imbalance between the poor and the rich—such shared ethical commitments give religious persons from differing backgrounds "new eyes" and "new ears" with which to see and understand one another. What is foreign in another religion can take on both depth and clarity when one grasps its meaning for the poor and its power to transform the world. Though starting with ethics, the kind of dialogue we are advocating with this book will lead to explicitly religious conversation because religious ethics are rooted in religious beliefs. Agreement on the level of ethical action raises, and helps answer, the question of possible agreement on the level of beliefs. In the process of what I have referred to elsewhere as "globally responsible dialogue," we can explore, and perhaps better understand, the earlier question of whether there is a common transcendent Reality within all the religions.[2]

The Poor as Mediators between the Religions and Students

If the poor can help the religions better understand one another, they can also, we believe, aid the so-called broad public to understand what religion is all about. I am speaking here about the many curious and concerned people who are broadly interested in religion, but who are also pointedly concerned about how we can make this world work better. Dr. Muzaffar and I, along with those associated with the Boston Research Center for the 21st Century, are convinced that this book opens the door to an engaging and effective way to study what in university/college course listings is often called "comparative religions." By shining a flashlight into the darkness of the sufferings and needs of the poor, which have in so many regions worsened during the era of globalization, our contributors have illuminated a variety of urgent questions. As they explore these questions in light of religious teachings, not only will students find themselves motivated to take up the exploration of religions, but they will be given some guidance in the evaluation of ideas and religious teachings that

[2] I try to describe such a "globally responsible dialogue" and its possible fruits in *One Earth Many Religions: Multifaith Dialogue and Global Responsibility* (Maryknoll, N.Y.: Orbis Books, 1995).

might otherwise be inaccessible to them. This connection of real-life concerns with religious ideals mirrors the same dynamic that we were talking about earlier in which the poor serve as mediators who introduce the religions to one another. By starting with an ethical response to real-world problems, we move into theology. Or better yet, practice illumines theory. By asking how the religions can alleviate suffering, students can better understand the teachings of the world religions.

And so we hope this collection of essays will serve as an effective college textbook or as a resource for adult-education courses. It could function as an additional text for courses that come under the general headings of "comparative religions," "comparative religious ethics," or "dialogue among religions." After the students have read and discussed the chapter(s) on a particular tradition in one of the many standard textbooks on "the religions of the world," they could, as it were, deepen what they have studied by reading the chapter in this book on how this particular religion is trying to respond to the challenges of global poverty. For more advanced or graduate courses, this collection might serve as the focal text; after reading a particular chapter, students would be invited to research and report on other sources, especially from the additional readings at the end of each chapter.

In teaching such courses, I have found that one way of engaging the students is to divide them, at the beginning of the semester, into groups in which individuals serve as spokespersons for a particular religion throughout the semester. Thus the "Hindu" or the "Jewish" students would be expected to represent these traditions and look for opportunities for dialogue as the class studies each of the other traditions. Always, though, the guiding question is: How can each religious tradition help us to better understand the economy and help remove, or diminish, the blight of poverty and injustice?

The Poor as Mediators between the Religions and Economics/Politics

Among the conversations that the poor of this world are mediating and facilitating for the religions of this world, perhaps the most urgent and the most telling will be the conversation between religion and economics. In this encounter, the poor are asking the religions for help. The present global market may constitute the most powerful economic engine that humans have ever put together. It may have generated over the past decade an amount of material growth and goods never before achieved in human history. It may have linked nations in mutual cooperation and dependence that only a century ago were inconceivable. All of this may be true, but from the perspective of the more than 1.3 billion people who earn less than a dollar a day, or the thirty-two thousand children who die daily of curable diseases, the global economy *is not working.* Something has to be done and help is needed from whoever might provide it.

As this book indicates, the religious traditions feel that they might be able to offer the kind of help that cannot be found, or cannot be delivered, anywhere else. This is not to say that the religions are presenting themselves as the saviors of the poor and the redeemers of the economy. If economic salvation is going to come, it will be the result of many different people and powers working together. But perhaps the contribution of the religions is an important, if not essential, ingredient in that cooperative mix. As the essays in this book make clear, the religions do feel that they offer wisdom and experience that is absolutely essential for any economic system to function and to achieve what most economic systems include among their fundamental goals: the well-being of everyone. But wisdom and values, it seems to many, have not played a role in the global economy as we know it; such wisdom is either not present in the global system, or it is not able to function, or it is not taken seriously by policy makers and business leaders. For the sake of the poor and the many who are not receiving the benefits of the burgeoning global market economy, the religions want to help.

This means that there needs to be a more vital and engaged dialogue between religious spokespersons and those who wield economic power. And there are good reasons to call this an "interreligious dialogue." By "interreligious" I mean religious communities on one side of the table and the global market on the other. Yes, I am suggesting that the market today is a religion! As one of the authors in this book has shown in another publication, in the way the market works and in the way it is presented to people, it evinces all the qualities that are usually associated with religion and religious claims (Loy 2000, 15-28). The basic beliefs or principles of present-day neoliberal economics are generally presented as dogma that one has to accept on faith and sometimes with a trust that looks like blind faith (e.g., "Trade must be free, with as little government intervention as possible."). The authority of the market is generally presented and accepted as absolute, even infallible (e.g., "Sorry, this is what the market dictates. We have to accept it."). Economists who interpret the mysteries and demands of the economy for us are often treated as "theologians" who know better than we what is good for us, or even as high-priests whose authority is unquestionable (e.g., "As Professor So-and-So of the University of Chicago tells us . . ."). And most tellingly, the present global, economic system is taken for granted as the only system, the only way the economy can work, the "one and only" way to achieve prosperity for all. If you are not part of it, you will be lost. "Outside the market, no salvation!"

Whether we are conscious of it or not, if the market is actually functioning as a religion, then it needs to enter into a dialogue with other religions. That's what this book is urging. But in order for such a dialogue to take place, the market-as-religion and the economists and politicians who stand behind it are going to have to accept for themselves what is required of all the other religions in order to engage in authentic dialogue. The global market and its captains are going to have to give up their claim to be the one and only religion, and they must relinquish their claim to the superior or absolute truth. If any one religion claims to be the only true religion, it can't really be part of a dialogue in which everyone is ready to learn from one another. That goes for Christianity as a religion and it goes for the market-place as a religion.

Our hope is that this book will promote real conversation, not only among the traditional religions, but also between the religions and the economy. We do not know the outcome, but we do know that this interreligious dialogue will be a conversation that can only be possible when everyone involved realizes that they have much to learn from one another.

AN OVERVIEW

All of the essays in this book, each in its own way and with particular emphases and concerns, show how the religions of the world are hearing the voices of the poor and, as a result, feel called to greater dialogue with one another, with economists and politicians, with anyone who wants to listen. Representing the primal religions—the oldest of all the traditions we will be hearing from—Ifi Amadiume speaks out of her knowledge and personal experience of the Igbo people in Africa. Her perspective is unique among those of this book in that it engagingly shows how the economic system of her people functioned in a tense interaction between matriarchy and patriarchy. The dialogue between gods and goddesses, between Earth and Sky, was not just religious but had definite payoff for how wealth and well-being were achieved and shared. With the coming of the European colonialists, the local patriarchs gained the upper hand, and here is where Amadiume draws some revealing conclusions that can inform the present global system.

Swami Agnivesh, reflecting both his knowledge of Hinduism and his social activism within the poverty and religious pluralism of India, offers a dialectical, good news/bad news perspective on the relationship between the religions and the economy. On the one hand, he is convinced that only a religious vision and transformation can counteract the greed that seems to propel the market; only when persons come to realize and feel that, as Hinduism tells us, we are all one family is there hope to transform the economic system. On the other hand, Agnivesh painfully recognizes that so much of institutional religion, in India and elsewhere, has sold out to those in power or is being exploited by them. A religious renewal is needed, and for that, interreligious dialogue and cooperation are essential.

From his study and practice of Buddhism, David Loy admits that in his essential teachings, Buddha does not endorse any one economic system. But he does clearly warn that no economic system can be divorced from values. More precisely, Buddhism warns that greed is part of the root cause of suffering; therefore any economy that does not control—or, worse, that promotes—greed is in trouble or will cause trouble. This does not mean that Buddhism is opposed to having and enjoying the goods of this world; it just warns that to really enjoy them, we must not cling to them. And, furthermore, we must share them. When the goods of this world are not shared equitably, as is presently the case, Buddha's first step toward a solution is not to call for *justice*, but rather, for *generosity* (*dana*). Our individual hearts must be transformed into hearts of compassion; only then is lasting justice possible.

From her immersion in Confucian studies and culture, and from her up-close view of the fruits of globalization in China, Zhou Qin first offers a lucid, incisive diagnosis of the present neoliberal economic system. Its "fundamental error," she believes, "lies in supposing that under the justification of unconditional competition, human society can be directed and improved by the rule of the free market alone." Rugged, competitive individualism is at the heart of the problem. But her suggested Confucian remedy does not simply absorb the individual into the community. Rather, the value and initiative of the individual person, family, nation are affirmed—but always in relationship to a sense of responsibility for and interdependence with the larger community. Thus, self-interest *is* other-interest, and vice versa. As Zhou Qin reminds us, to know, feel, and live this truth of Confucian ethics will "change the rules" of the present global economic game.

Moving our vision from East to West, from Asian to so-called Abrahamic religious perspectives, rabbi and Jewish scholar Norman Solomon first warns us that to invoke the Jewish Bible as an endorsement of any particular economic system (capitalism or socialism) is to read more *into* the sacred text than *out of* it. The Bible does not favor one system over the other. But, according to Rabbi Solomon, it does insist that for any economic system to achieve its goals, it must be animated and guided by justice and compassion. For practically minded Jews, Solomon reminds us, such virtues must be translated into clear guidelines and laws, for Judaism recognizes realistically that the "good" of pursuing wealth will always expose us to the "evil inclination" of greed. He gives examples from Jewish history of how the rabbis through the ages tried to make sure that greed never overpowered justice and compassion. And he suggests that these examples can serve as paradigms for our present global economy.

Sallie McFague, one of the most respected voices in the Christian discussion of what the gospel means for ecology and economy, believes that the witness of Jesus in the New Testament does enable, even requires, Christians to choose between economic systems. She first analyzes two such systems: the dominant *neoclassical market model*, with its goal of promoting human well-being through ever greater growth and consumption, and the *ecological economic model*, with its creed of interdependence and its goal of planetary sustainability. Admitting that most Christians in North America would probably line up behind the market model, she makes her case that if Christians take seriously what Jesus envisioned by the Kingdom of God, they will have to change their economic loyalties and practices. That would make not only for a more authentic Christian life but also for a more just and sustainable world. McFague is also convinced that in pursuing what Jesus intended by the Kingdom of God, his followers will find many dialogue partners in other religions.

Ameer Ali would be one such dialogue partner. Perhaps because he is an economist by profession, as well as a Muslim by confession, his essay stands out from the others in this book in its extensive description and analysis of the global economic system. In the way the global market is functioning and in the economic disparity and poverty it either allows or engenders, Ali finds a stark contrast with Islam's view of both human nature and human society. According to the Qur'an, neither politics nor economics can ever be removed from religious values and ethics. And according to Islamic ethics, "there is no place in Islam either for individual self-interest or for the market forces to enjoy unrestricted freedom. . . . Islam is not against profit motive, the cardinal principle of free market ideology, but it is not willing to allow profit motive to determine human progress." Ali admits the discrepancy between such ideals and actual practice in many Muslim countries, and he suggests how ideals and practices can be brought closer, for Islam and for the world.

In his concluding commentary, coeditor Chandra Muzaffar takes up the difficult, but important, task of asking whether the different religious voices we have heard in these essays might make for a chorus. In their different diagnoses of the global market, in the varying remedies that they draw from their own traditions, can they "sing together"? Of course, singing together would not mean singing the same tune. Whatever harmony might be possible, it would be polyphonic. Do the religions offer a polyphonic, contrasting yet harmonizing, message for those who are in charge of the global economic system and/or for those who are struggling to understand or reform it? Can the religious communities of the world form any kind of a common front from which to engage the global market? There is no definitive answer to such questions. Muzaffar's conclusion is more of an invitation to continue the exploration, which will be possible only if we continue the dialogue between religions and economics—a dialogue that the poor of our earth are not only urging, but demanding.

Chapter 1

Igbo and African Religious Perspectives on Religious Conscience and the Global Economy

By Ifi Amadiume

Abstract

This essay uses an analysis and critique of Igbo tradition to address the historical dispute between indigenous matriarchy (decentralization, peace, and equity) and the historical development of patriarchy (centralization, greed, violence, and imperialism). Central to this analysis is the primordial gendered power dispute between Earth and Sky as this translates into biographies of gods and goddesses in their religious and civil status in the context of a political economic theory. Thus, the essay presents a dialogue about gods and goddesses as a paradigmatic contestation of truths, and argues the presence of a primordial pluralism with historical consequences for our experiences of morals, ethics, civility, rights, social justice, and happiness.

In a cross-cultural comparative study, informed by class, race, and gender perspectives, the essay demonstrates how ideas embedded in the Igbo history of gender and material culture relate to Africa's experiences of the problems of greed, imperialism, and the global economy. The essay points to two important conclusions: (1) the importance of gender perspectives to enable us to capture more fully the cultural and social dynamism involved in religious beliefs and the global political economy, and (2) by extension the importance of a gender dimension to theory and method in the study of religions in Africa. Finally, the essay addresses lessons that can be learned from Igbo and African traditions in interreligious dialogue and economic justice in our global system.

Introduction

Africa is the second largest continent in the world, encompassing 11,724,000 square miles. Life began and has continued unbroken in Africa since the beginning of human existence. With such a deep and complex history, it is impossible to present a pure African religious tradition or a simple perspective on religious conscience and economic theory and principles. Africa does not have a single religious tradition or even a single culture. There is no text such as a Bible or Qur'an that all Africans abide by. African traditions, therefore, present some challenges. In Africa, we are faced with diverse religions—almost as many as the various ethnic societies and languages of precolonial and traditional Africa. In Africa, we have practitioners of indigenous religions as well as followers of Islam and Christianity. We also have followers of Hinduism and Judaism in East Africa and in the southern African countries. Such diversity is not surprising because Africa has more than 3,000 ethnic groups and 2,100 languages.

To address the topic of *Subverting Greed*, I have chosen to present a dialectical analysis and critique of traditional Igbo religious ideas and economic principles. I will present Igbo ideas in relation to other African traditions in wider African and global contexts informed by gender, class, and race perspectives. I will also use a combination of theories and methods, which I have previously applied in my work, that relate meaning and material power to social values and social history (Ifi Amadiume 1987; 1997). In this essay, the Igbo political economy is examined to form a basis for a critique of the theory of free market economics.

Igbo societies developed along strong matriarchal foundations that gave prominence to females, especially women as mothers who headed matricentric (mother-focused) households. The female-focused household formed the primary production unit in the kinship system in which mothers and household members worked for the economic self-sufficiency of the matricentric household. Families and lineages headed by males were grafted onto matricentric households through marriage. There was a later development of patriarchy which has been associated with the colonial state and a capitalist economy. There is also evidence of precolonial patriarchy. This particular social order might be characterized by its accumulation and monopolization of capital resources, especially land, and the religion of ancestors controlled by male elders that was precapitalist and based on lineage. I distinguish lineage patriarchy from the state-sanctioned patriarchy that came later with colonialism because these two kinds of patriarchy had very different impacts on local economies and social relations.

In this analysis of the Igbo tradition, I will specifically address the historical dispute or conflict between indigenous matriarchy and the historical development of patriarchy since these two distinct systems have embodied contrasting social values and economic principles. I will explore this juxtaposition of matriarchy and patriarchy in Igbo tradition as evidence of early pluralism in the indigenous society. From the dawn of history matriarchy has had an ameliorating influence on patriarchy in West Africa and was, therefore, an alternative socioeconomic theory that stood in opposition to patriarchy. My study of the Igbo and a comparison with several societies in Africa have led me to contrast matriarchal social values such as decentralization, peace, and equity with patriarchy, which has generated centralization, greed, violence, and imperialism. These contrasting approaches to economic practice are relevant for our understanding of Africa's contemporary experiences with the problems of greed, imperialism, and the global economy. From an understanding of the links between social values and economic systems, we can draw lessons from the Igbo and African experiences that are useful in an interreligious understanding of economic justice today.

Theory and Method: Gender, Ideology, and Truths

Wim van Binsbergen and Matthew Schoffeleers, working from the premise that "People's myths do not function at the metaphysical level alone" (van Binsbergen and Schoffeleers 1985, 21), pose an interesting question about Wauthier de Mahieu's study of two contrasting myths of the origin of circumcision among the Komo of Zaire. They point out that it is not enough to simply relate the cultural meaning of myths to specific social groups. It is also necessary to look at historical and social contradictions (de Mahieu 1985, 21).

Groups in society are involved in social relations. The existence of two circumcision myths of the Komo instead of one could be explained in relation to an internal power struggle and changes in relations of production in Komo society. Yet, that this power struggle could be about different gender ideologies and economic theories with structural and historical implications for the study of African traditional religions does not enter the imagination of these male scholars.[1] I have mentioned the presence of contrasting theories of matriarchy and patriarchy in Igbo tradition above. Thus, my analysis of the struggle for primacy between contrasting myths in Igbo thought places religious pluralism (where people are exposed to more than one religious tradition and values) at the origins of the world. The world here obviously means the world of the Igbo and the beginning of their society, long before the presence of Christian missionary and colonial imperialism in Africa.

In traditional Igbo thought there is a theoretical and moral argument about cultural values and economic principles between *Ala* (Earth)[2] and *Elu* (Sky),[3] which, respectively, represent female and male energy. A similar tradition exists among neighboring peoples and other West African societies. With these spiritual forces in mind, I wish to demonstrate the dynamic connections between ideas, theory, religious beliefs, economic principles, and sociopolitical practice. In this context, politics means that sacred ideas take on gender characteristics. Such a view of politics includes analyses of biographies of gods and goddesses and their civil status. I am, therefore, presenting a dialogue about gods and goddesses as a contest of truths that becomes a paradigm for how the entire society approaches social issues. The argument between Earth and Sky is a dialogue between two views of society with significant consequences for our experiences of morals, ethics, civility, rights, social justice, and happiness.

The Igbo Principle of Equality

The Igbo-speaking people of Nigeria live in their traditional homeland and in diverse countries of the world (Ifi Amadiume

[1] These editors of a seminal work on African religions were honest enough to write, "None of our contributors is African, and none is a woman. At the level of abstraction that is maintained in this collection, this state of affairs may not have led to dramatic distortions" (van Binsbergen and Schoffeleers 1985, 37). They, however, admit that the presence of such "colleagues" would have been beneficial. The intellectual and political shortcomings are enormous, owing to such an omission of women's voices that seems so common in religious studies.

[2] *Ala* in Southern Igbo dialect; *Ani* in Northern Igbo dialect.

[3] *Elu* in Southern Igbo dialect; *Enu* in Northern Igbo dialect.

1995). They are more than 30 million in population and have one of the highest population densities in West Africa. Igbo subcultures are distributed in six ecological zones. Linguistically, Igbo, which is spoken in West Africa, is one of the *Kwa* subgroups of the Niger–Congo language family. While there are many dialects, I will use Igbo words interchangeably, paying little attention to strict consistency of dialect.

The Igbo propose a binary principle as expressed in the statement *Ihe di abuo abuo,* or "things exist in pairs," which suggests a deep belief in the principle of equality that is related to balancing contrasting or opposing forces. There is a similar statement, *Ife kwulu, ife akwudobe ya,* whose literal translation is, "something else always stands beside something," which means that there are no absolutes, nor is there absolute truth.[4] Furthermore, the Igbo have an axiomatic statement, *Ana bu isi* in Northern Igbo dialect, which means, "Earth is senior" or "Earth is first." From the Southern Igbo dialect there is a counter-proposition in the name of an oracle called *Igwe ka Ala,* which claims the seniority of Sky to Earth.

Looking at these statements, we see a problem in that the Igbo propose an ideal of equality, yet social process demonstrates a contradiction in social relations in claims and counterclaims to primordial seniority. For example, the Igbo word for "human" is a genderless *Nmadu,* "person," yet in Igbo societies a powerful goddess is often said to have a husband, and this leads to a debate about which deity or gender has seniority over the other. In Nnobi, a village ward where the god Aho dwells claims that the

[4] Chike Aniakor and Herbert Cole use the term "dualism," which they describe as "the dynamic relationships between opposites" (Aniakor and Cole 1984, 17). They translate the proverb *Ihe di abuo* as "Things are in twos." Also, for their version *Ihe kwuru ihe akwudebe ya,* their translation is, "When something stands, something [else] stands beside it." They write, "We see this as the reflection of an ancient and deep-seated Igbo dualistic pattern of thought. While binary oppositions . . . obviously exist everywhere, our contention here is that they operate more explicitly in Igbo thinking than among other African peoples" (ibid.) Also, their translation of the proverb *Okilikili bu ije agwo* is, "Circular, circular is the snake's path." They explain this further to have a more figurative meaning, "Things happen in cycles," and give examples of cyclical interactions between the living and the dead as, for example, reincarnation (ibid. 1984, 18).

powerful goddess Idemili is the wife of the lesser deity Aho. The village ward where Idemili is located disputes this claim. Such disputes are invariably linked to the order of rights and privileges of spouses, village wards, and priests to officiate in ritual and ceremonies or in the redistribution of food and material goods. We can, thus, understand that this is a dialogic contest—or argument—about the metaphors used to describe society: Earth (female) in opposition to Sky (male). In short, the contest is about how to represent culture. The dispute about seniority raises the question of which gender has the capacity for inclusiveness. All this allows for male and female views in the story of origins and the source of power in the world.

Understandably, earth as the source of all life has many proponents. Regarding the production of food, on which we depend, Igbo say, "The 'earth force' is great . . . there was a covenant between earth and man. . . . The earth becomes the greatest supernatural force (*alusi*). . . . No person should defile the earth by spilling human blood in violence on it. This is the covenant" (Nwaokoye Odenigbo, aged 83, in Isichei 1978, 22-23). In her book entitled *Igbo Worlds: An Anthology of Oral Histories and Historical Descriptions*, Elizabeth Isichei writes, "The fertility of the land made no difference to the reverence with which it was regarded. *Ana*, the divine Earth, has a key role in Igbo religion, reflecting the values of an agricultural community. Many offenses were regarded as abominable, not so much in themselves, but because they offended her" (Isichei 1978, 27). Thus, in Igbo tradition the Earth goddess is the most important deity, the guardian of morality, and the controller of the economy.

The Igbo are not alone among African peoples who acknowledge earth as a paradigm of life and culture. Neighbors of the Igbo hold similar philosophies as, for example, the Idoma people for whom Earth worship was the only all-embracing public religious rite (Armstrong 1982, 7). The later importance of the concept of a god above earth was traced to the influence of Islam, which spread from northern Nigeria to the Benue region around the thirteenth century. With the onset of centralized power there was much more abstraction and masculinization of religious objects and references. Matters such as the worship of earth and woman were seen as pagan concerns, something belonging to the era of ignorance (according to Islam) and darkness (according to Christianity).

In spite of the overwhelming evidence of a matriarchal theory and the many Igbo male and female deities, efforts are still made by Igbo Christian theologians to reduce religion to the single truth of a supreme male God. The reason is that priests and theologians have dominated the study of Igbo religion and have represented ideas in Igbo traditions through Christian thought. Such a false claim against the facts of traditional pluralism justifies patriarchal greed, totalitarian patriarchy, gender oppression, and centrism. However, the promulgation of these values required a negation of the traditional matriarchal system of knowledge. They also facilitated the triumph of imperialism, social and civil injustice, and human unhappiness, all of which are manifested by neoliberal global capitalism.

Igbo Political Economy and the "Economic Theory" of African Traditional Religions

Classical economics views the individual as "economic man," a rational being out to maximize his self-interest. This theory would stand if economics could stand alone. Yet in social practice, economics is integrated in other social institutions. Economics belongs within a sociocultural context or else there would be no means of communicating or understanding economic behavior. All human beings exist within societies and cultures with different expressions of inequality and choice, depending on age, gender, class, and race. Economics is about culture, and culture continuously reinvents what is to be considered ethical and unethical economic exchange, which is where greed comes into the picture.

History shows that most sociocultural systems do not support greed and avarice. There are societies such as the Igbo where principles of exchange were determined by social values and kinship ethics, thus taking the discourse on greed beyond the question of scarcity and affluence. However, under the specific conditions that existed during the slave trade (fifteenth to nineteenth century) and colonialism (late nineteenth to mid-twentieth century) that devastated and arrested Africa's development, greed was encouraged and forced on natives. Thus, we must integrate Africa's historical experiences of the connections between gender, greed, violence, and corruption that were imposed by external forces with internal, gender-conscious, social systems that had been in place for generations. If we acknowledge that economic systems exist within a social context, we must accept the importance of considering the political economy of greed from the perspective of gender and power.

Many precolonial communities in Africa, even those under kings, queens, and chiefs, were decentralized in a political system that favored more participation in religion, social events, economic production, and decision-making by kinship groups, local associations of women's groups, and citizens in general. These systems emphasized traditional pluralism, shared kinship, community, and human oneness. In precolonial Igbo societies, kinship morality that stipulated appropriate conduct between relatives and social rules saw land as unexchangeable wealth. This is why precolonial Igbo societies are not considered capitalist. In the economic and religious practice of Igbo tradition, land maps contained the names or symbols of dead forebears and ancestors and, therefore, land was not within the sphere of market exchange because land was never to be alienated. Yet, to see land in this way is to focus on the power of lineage or village elders who controlled the accumulation and distribution of capital goods such as land, cattle, and women as the means of production. It was the corruption of this patriarchal class by colonial powers that resulted in the greed of the lineage elders in collaboration with totalitarian state patriarchy. The combination of these internal and external patriarchal forces worked against the traditional matriarchal system and resulted in gender oppression.

In the indigenous matriarchal ideology of an Igbo society like the Nnobi people, eating together and sharing one womb was spoken of as *Umunne,* the closest unit of kinship, the matricentric unit (Amadiume 1987; 1997). The literal translation of *Umunne* is "children of mother, " and it is the Igbo term for siblings. The same term is used for much wider categories of relatives in the lineage. All members of society were children of one mother who ate out of one pot, bound by the spirit of common motherhood. The application and relevance of this theory beyond the matricentric unit to a wider superstructure showed a connection between the matricentric production unit, the economy, and culture. This basic theory was reproduced at wider levels of social organization in the political structure. All Nnobi people were children of one mother, the goddess Idemili, worshipped by all Nnobi people. This relational matriarchal model governed the logic of village administration through a four-day market system in civil society. The names of the four market days were also the names of the days of the week and the names of goddesses. As markets were held in honor of these goddesses, economics and culture were integrated into a holistic system.

Parallel to the dialogue between Earth and Sky in the Igbo dual-sex, sociopolitical system, a matriarchal system was in dialectical relationship to a patriarchal system. There was also a mediating third system. This third holistic system was based on a nongendered collective humanity, *Nmadu* ("person, human"). This holistic system can only have been based on a relational matriarchal model growing out of the interconnection of economics, religion, and culture based on the goddess Idemili of Nnobi. She provided a unifying moral code and culture that communicated the theory of a common motherhood. In this way, the goddess Idemili generated affective relationships. People bargained with several religious and cultural systems, and this is what I interpret as traditional pluralism in which a matriarchal theory presents an alternative socioeconomic model to the narrow choice presented by patriarchy.

But economic exchange was not the only way in which matriarchy shaped society. Igbo traditions and those of many societies in Africa are rich in data on rites of passage, especially initiation rituals. Apart from food production and marketing, one of the major activities of traditional women's associations was girls' initiation schools, where moral virtues and aesthetic ideals for responsible citizenship were taught. These places for the generation and teaching of women's cultures helped introduce into society alternative ethics that did not idealize war and blood and the valor of killing. If there was any "violence," it was done to the "self" in contexts where females were tested and trained in ordeals of courage and endurance and blessed by female spirits and goddesses. In this kind of socialization for citizenship, the religious is not separate from economic, legal, social, or environmental ethics.

Igbo women equated colonial invasion and conquest of their lands to the dying of their own bodies. Not surprisingly, Igbo women and neighboring Ibibio women fought the anticolonial Women's War of 1929, led by matriarchs against the economic, cultural, religious, and political marginalization of women and the destabilizing effects of monetary changes, taxation, and a cash-crop economy. In traditional Igbo thought, all things have a living soul and—like the body of a woman—if you overuse, you kill. This is a good lesson for environmental ethics, as we now know that our environmental resources are not infinite.

In Igbo societies, women's active and intensive involvement in production was a means to wealth that was independent of a marital or patriarchal control based on lineage. A women's culture of organizations, associations, prestige societies, and goddesses provided a social and public opportunity for women to convert wealth into prestigious roles and titles and become social and political leaders of their community. They were able to limit greed by redistributing their wealth through the expansion of their household, using socially approved institutions. Women also limited greed through social ceremonies and festivals that required public feasting. Male elders were more likely to keep their wealth for themselves and were more often accused of self-aggrandizement. Women have continued with some of these traditions of matriarchy into the postcolonial societies as they use their resources and wealth for the general well-being of their families and communities. Yet they are still fighting money, men, the state and—these days—the World Bank and the International Monetary Fund (IMF) to preserve the social character of the marketplace, which is the Igbo woman's second home.

What are the modern and interfaith lessons to be learned from this Igbo political economy and goddess configuration? Present-day Igbo women have translated and reconfigured some of this tradition into churchwomen's associations and guilds of wives and mothers. However, patriarchal Christian gender biases have narrowed the open access that women formerly had to their Town Women's Councils. In traditional religion, all town women automatically belonged to the Town Women's Council and had strong involvement in the management of the marketplace. The church and Christian denominations have divided Igbo women, who had been united under this strong ideology and culture of women's economic solidarity. For example, churchwomen's organizations separate economics from religion and limit their membership to only "morally approved" women who are married under the blessing of the church, those who have had a Christian wedding in the appropriate denomination. The marketplace, trading, and goddess culture united and empowered Igbo women of earlier generations and, by association, Igbo society.

Postcolonial Market Forces

From the late nineteenth century to the middle of the twentieth century, strict adherence to the traditional cultural rules of exchange and exchange value broke down under colonialism. New forms of exchange empowered lineage patriarchy, for it was this segment of society that was enriched by the transformation of currency that was introduced in the early twentieth century by the colonial government. The use of money instead of trade by barter, reciprocal exchange, and minimal use of cumbersome mediums of exchange such as beads, cowrie shells, and salt and iron rods introduced new market principles as natives were coerced into adopting modern market principles that forever altered previously differentiated exchange categories, reducing almost everything to market value, including women, who now had to be married with a designated "bride price." The imposition of tax on the natives by the colonial government led to the need for cash, which in turn led to a cash-crop economy, labor migration, and land alienation. By encouraging a competitive and fragmented culture, these processes supported a patriarchal path to development.

Today, women work the land and are more involved in agriculture, food processing, trade, and marketing than the men who now control or own land. These contradictions have created age and gender tensions as well as individual anxiety over access, succession, and inheritance due to the likelihood of abuse of power by male elders. Many religions still worship ancestors and, from the point of view of social justice for women, ancestor worship can be seen as a negative aspect of traditional religions in Africa. After all, ancestor worship was the ideological basis for lineage patriarchy, which tended to accumulate and monopolize capital goods. I have mentioned that precolonial lineage patriarchy was not usually considered a capitalist economy as there was no alienation of land or presence of a monetary economy. Men *did* tend toward patriarchal abuse of power, but traditional matriarchy had an ameliorating influence on lineage patriarchy through a system of checks and balances that were a part of the culture. Thus, unlike other cultures and religions, precolonial lineage patriarchy did not develop into full feudalism because of a political economy of collective ownership of wealth and the strong presence of the relational matriarchal model (Amadiume 1997).

Postcolonial Igbo political economy operates within a sociocultural context that is local yet also extends beyond Igbo borders to the national, regional, international, and global scene. Igbo market systems constitute several internal and external markets that link many Igbo villages, but extend to wider exchange and distribution networks. These market systems operate on a combination of sociocultural values that are subjected to the dictates of market forces at the national and international level.

The postcolonial state also has tried to undermine women's strong control of the marketplace and erode the informal sector of the economy in the name of development through various "modernization" measures that have not benefited the general populace. As traditional women have suffered all this intrusion on their market space by greed and the state, they have also suffered under the sexist policies of Structural Adjustment measures by the World Bank and the International Monetary Fund that have created dependency, new class divisions, and corruption.

Lessons of Greed in Local Thought, Folklore, and Literature

The ameliorating influence of matriarchy is important in emphasizing Igbo women's struggle against patriarchy and women's strategies of resistance against market forces. I have argued that it is the relational matriarchal model that contains the ideal economic theory of African traditional religions; this is a theory of community, exchange, reciprocity, and sharing. This relational matriarchal theory is based on the ideology of *Umunne*, those who share the spirit of common motherhood, who eat out of one pot, and are bound by the prohibition of *Ibenne*, a taboo of same blood where love and not self-interest rules. Thus as relatives they must be truthful, trusting, and loving to one another. They should never cheat one another. Social values of exchange are better expressed in matriarchy than in lineage patriarchy because patriarchy promotes competition rather than exchange. A brief consideration of the stories common to Igbo culture will reveal the sources of matriarchal economic principles and lessons of greed in local thought.

Folklorists of Africa have analyzed myths, proverbs, folktales, and rituals. This work shows that religion is not a separate institution and has no monopoly on moral and ethical ideas. Like economics, religion is integrated in culture. Although folklore is often seen as local tales told by the illiterate or peasant classes, folklore also contains popular opinion coded in myths against rigid official positions, the larger symbolic stories that function as mirrors of human experience. William Bascom (Bascom 1972) has argued that African "dilemma tales" are narratives with no easy answers demanding moral and ethical judgments. These tales pose tough choices between alternatives and encourage debate and argument. A parallel can be drawn to the myth of the quarrel between Earth and Sky, a struggle to define origins and a representation of culture from the perspective of gender.

Folklore is, in fact, where women's voices can best be heard, especially in the evenings, at the end of a hard day's work, telling moral stories against greed, selfishness, envy, and injustice.

Women tell these stories while they continue to do more leisurely work, such as shelling seeds and nuts or grating tubers or even plaiting hair (Amadiume 1987). This legacy is captured in popular African novels in which mothers tell animal and nature stories, while fathers and *griots*[5] tell bloody epic stories of war, valor, and violence in fights for succession to political office, as two popular epics, *Sundiata* and *Nwindo,* demonstrate.

Contemporary African writers have also been dealing with the theme of greed as a means of showing how the current economic system leads to political corruption and social problems. Compared to male writers, Igbo women writers like Flora Nwapa and Buchi Emecheta are radical messengers; they have focused on the domestic violence against women that results from marriage and patriarchal greed. In all Nwapa's work, especially in *Efuru* (1966), the wayward Water goddess, Mammy Water, is the icon of self-repossessed female sexuality, choice, material wealth, and hard-won freedom. In Emecheta's two novels, *The Joys of Motherhood* (1979) and *Kehinde* (1994), women experience similar patriarchal oppression and domestic violence.

Thus, metaphors, ideas, customs, values, and motifs in folktales continue to feed the minds of even European-trained African creative writers, who also pass on traditional stories and proverbs beyond their African origins. Tales may be local, but their moral lessons are shared African universals such as, "one should not reward good/kindness with wickedness and ingratitude," "there is no reward in crime," and "greed is punished." In these modern tales both the victim and the perpetrator of injustice suffer.

There are also shared universals in proverbs. Oral tradition is rich in sayings about sharing, reciprocity, redistribution, and community—strong economic principles of the relational matriarchal model of African traditional religions. This is captured in the Igbo proverb *Egbe belu, Ugo belu; nkesilu ibe ya ebena, mkwu kwakwa ya,* "Let the hawk perch; let the eagle perch as well; a bird

[5] A *griot* is the professional and official oral historian. In many societies in Africa there were no written records and names of dynasties. Important events and traditions were memorized, recited, and passed on by the *griots,* who had to follow strict rules so that their recitations were mostly the official version of history.

that refuses another to perch may it lose its wings." Thus, judgment is pronounced on extreme selfishness. To emphasize the principle of gender equality Igbo say, *Osa na nkwu, uze na nkwu, afo rie ya chaara ibe ya.* The literal translation is, "Male squirrel on palm-tree, female squirrel on palm-tree, whichever eats some fruits should give chance to the other." This might be explained as, "Let us observe the policy of live and let live" (Solomon Amadiume 1995, 29).

In these oral expressions of justice, greed is regarded as almost evil. Specific animals symbolize capitalist greed and the exploitation of the masses. For example, the vulture, a dominant image in films and folktales, conveys cannibalism and scavenging. Similarly, in Djibril Diop Mambety's film about Senegal, *Hyenas* (1992), hyenas and witches cannibalizing the poor symbolize African elites as agents of Western materialism. In East Africa, the hyena is seen to resemble the character of a murderous and cannibalistic witch (Beidelman 1961, 61-74; 1963, 54-69). In ChiChewa, a Malawian language, greed is *Umbombo*, and anyone practicing it would be regarded as very cruel (a witch or sorcerer). In Sudan the "hyena-man" tales are about a monstrous, hyena-like creature that terrorizes the countryside. This monster is not only outside ordered and cultured society but also represents the chaotic aspect of a person (Calame-Griaule 1961, 89-118).

The anti-greed ethic is further illustrated by the proverb, *Erimala bu nkwu na ukwa, a dighi atakere ala atakere,* which translates as "The benefits of a piece of land are the economic trees therein, nobody eats the soil." The explanation of this proverb is, "Let one be content with the little one has" (Solomon Amadiume 1995, 54). Clearly, folk wisdom carries profound attitudes toward economic justice that are as relevant today as they have been for generations.

Greed, Economic Injustice, and the Postcolonial Global Economic Order

African countries are at a disadvantage in the present neoliberal global economic order. Governments are overburdened by cyclical debt and the social and economic degeneration that results from stringent Structural Adjustment Programs (SAP) imposed on them by the World Bank through the International Monetary Fund (IMF). The situation is not simply that of financial relations between lender and borrower. These external financial institutions, informed by neoliberalism, are meddling in the actual running of the government; they plan the development of so-called indebted African states, determine economic plans, and allocate budgets. By controlling economic policies, they perpetuate a neocolonialist policy of foreign economic and political domination that alienates African people from their indigenous ways and wisdom. In the international economic system, global financial institutions and trade organizations such as the World Trade Organization (WTO) and the Free Trade Area of the Americas (FTAA) are dominated by the rich countries. The policies of these growth-driven financial organizations and major agreements by trading partners, constituted by meetings of leaders of the rich countries known as the Group of Seven (G7) and the Group of Eight (G8), have been recognized as agents of global economic inequality (Mwaria et al. 2000).[6] In Africa, more money is spent on servicing debts than nation building. Developing countries need to use their money for social development rather than servicing a cyclical debt that never ends.

About forty years ago, on the eve of the independence of many African nations from colonial rule, the great humanist revolutionary Frantz Fanon condemned European global domination in no uncertain words when he wrote, "Let us waste no time in sterile litanies and nauseating mimicry. Leave this Europe where they are never done talking of Man, yet murder men everywhere they find them, at the corner of every one of their own streets, in all the corners of the globe. For centuries they have stifled almost the whole of humanity in the name of so-called spiritual experience. Look at them today swaying between atomic and spiritual disintegration" (Fanon 1963, 311).

There is no doubt that international capitalism has undermined indigenous values of self-reliance and self-sustaining devel-

[6] In particular, chapters in Mwaria's book by Dennis Brutus, George Caffentzis, Silvia Federici, and Karim Hirji are relevant to this point.

opment, particularly among women. Sexist policies on development such as an export cash-crop economy and uneconomic, donor-imposed "white elephant" projects resulting in debt for African governments have focused on men, with a negative effect on gender relations in local communities. Igbo women are waging a struggle against male, state, and external donor intervention as well as against policy reforms that are commodifying the marketplace, agricultural production, and rural development. So-called modernization policies are eroding the central role that women played in providing alternatives in the traditional economy and the development of their towns and villages (Amadiume 2000). In multiple donor-funded irrigation land distribution programs in Gambia, World Bank technical assistance and credit for increased agricultural production in Kenya, and similar projects in Ghana, women have found themselves and their labor placed under male management (Staudt 1995, 225-38). In this way, neoliberal economic policies are eroding traditional systems of complementary gender and economic cooperation that had been derived from the traditional relational matriarchal model described above.

Furthermore, poverty and hunger have directly been linked to the HIV/AIDS epidemic, while greed has also been responsible for the indifference and the lack of a coordinated effort to meet this emergency of catastrophic proportions. The statistics of unending mass deaths of black Africans are shattering. More than seventy percent—that is 25.3 million—of the 36 million adults and children living with HIV/AIDS in the world are in Black Africa or sub-Saharan Africa, which suggests a racial divide in the AIDS epidemic.[7] Seventeen million Africans have died of AIDS, including more than 3.7 million children. Twelve million African children are without parents because of AIDS. Meanwhile, local African people see multinational and pharmaceutical companies

[7] There are 400,000 infected people in North Africa/Middle East and 920,000 in North America, where, again, there is a racializing of infection with more annual new infections among black people (Haney, October 6, 2001a: B1). In spite of its comparatively low statistics of infection, in the U.S., the Center for Disease Control and Prevention spent $600 million per year on AIDS prevention (Haney, February 7, 2001b: B1).

as proverbial "hyenas" and "vultures" feeding off masses of the living dead with meager donations and expensive drugs, which only scratch the surface of this massive epidemic. Intervention in such a tragic pandemic should not be subject to market forces.[8]

Postcolonial Eurocentric ideals for development in Africa introduced the separation between religion, economics, and social life and principles that support human domination over nature and the separation of humans from other living things. African traditional religious thought would see the global economic principles that are operational today as emanating from the mechanical worldview of those without totem, those without taboos or ritual restrictions. Traditional Africans believe that the spiritual upheavals in Africa today emanate from the introduction of bad spirits; these bad spirits pollute the environment, pollute the mind, and waste lives. Local beliefs articulate the many faces of the political economy of globalization, class exploitation, poverty, and social afflictions.

Economic Justice and the Global System: Sharing and Conscience

We have demonstrated that the Igbo relational matriarchal model is an ameliorating force against greed because of the moral conscience of the principle of *Umunne* in which the children of one mother are bound in the spirit of common motherhood. This same force translates into the solidarity of clan, village, and nation. Related and unrelated Igbo groups far beyond their native villages have used the ideology of *Umunne* to forge a solidarity of trust. Traders and businesspeople have also used the matriarchal ideology of *Umunne* and have sealed deals with the oath of *Ibenne*. Matriarchy and the spirit of common motherhood make it possible to forge this relationship of love and trust by those who believe in the equality and sanctity of eating out of one pot. Igbo tradi-

[8] Defensive as drug manufacturers are about their response to the AIDS epidemic in Africa, between 10,000 and 25,000 Africans—fewer than .001 percent of those infected with HIV/AIDS—are receiving anti-retroviral medicines, according to UNAIDS figures.

tional religion of the relational matriarchal model can bring this rich gender-informed legacy to interreligious dialogue.

All the major religious traditions claim a community of faith. It would be interesting to compare how these notions of community deal with the important question of inclusiveness, equity, and gender justice. How does the notion of "children of God" in the Christian religion translate to the ideology of *Umunne*, the closest bond of love that is ritualized or sealed in the prohibition of *Ibenne*, which binds *Umunne* in a relationship of love and trust. How can interreligious dialogue embrace the Igbo notion of the sacredness of the mother and her unlimited authority to reform a patriarchal priesthood for the twenty-first century?

The Muslim religion has the concept of the community of Muslims, *Ummah*, which includes both men and women. Yet in practice both the Caliphate and the Imamate are rigidly hierarchical in gender and exclude women in the hierarchy of Imam. In Islam, patriarchal greed translates to a noninclusive family of men. What lessons can the followers of Islam learn from the relational matriarchal model that can be used to make better use of an Arab saying that claims "the mother is a school"? There is a similar statement in the sayings of the Muslim prophet Muhammad that is usually rendered as, "Paradise lies at the feet of mothers." Muslims need to do more than to understand these statements as injunctions to cherish and respect one's own mother.

Likewise, similar questions can be asked of the assumptions of a global community in the new world order. It is an Igbo religious concept that the mother gives her children and society the gift of *ite uba*, "the pot of prosperity," or material wealth and knowledge, so that all of her children can eat out of one pot. Who qualifies to eat out of one pot in the global community? Who qualifies for justice? In what ways can the alternative presented by a relational matriarchal model heal the wounds of the past and humanize society for the twenty-first century?

Our common humanity compels a commitment to global human rights and economic justice as children of one mother, *Umunne*. The problem is, of course, deep and complex even as all the traditions acknowledge that evil often triumphs over good. Igbo traditional religion does not preach perfection at all times but recognizes human weakness and occasional greed. Sometimes, deception and fraud may triumph: in Igbo allegories, even the tortoise can outwit the leopard. *Chi* is an Igbo concept of conscience that juxtaposes self-determination and destiny. When one has *Chi*, one is always in conversation and negotiation with one's *Chi*, one's conscience, or—in faith terms—one's spirit or divine self or spirit double. This juxtaposition of choice and fate in Igbo thought leaves room for personal creativity and social responsibility.

There are checks and balances in the strong emphasis that African religions place on sharing, tolerance, witnessing, forgiveness and reconciliation, conscience, and a life of transparency. Igbo say that one's neighbor is one's *Chi*. Thus, a deeper sense of shared humanity is encoded in the Igbo term for "fellow human being," which is *Nmadu-ibem*. Whereas in Western thought and ethics the female exists outside an androcentric humanity, Igbo's genderless *Nmadu-ibem* implies a complete mirror or replica of self, recognizing a common humanity that supercedes gender. Difference is respected by the fact that we each have our individual *Chi*. Even siblings of one mother each have a different creator, as the Igbo say, *Otu nne na-amu ma otu Chi anaghi eke*. This is explained as "a reference to people of the same parent but different talents" (Solomon Amadiume 1995, 63). This implies that each person's talents have a different source.

We can learn the lessons of an inclusive community from the Igbo relational matriarchal model. But a just society also depends on an ethic of sharing. African religions can contribute a deep sense of community through the universal concept of sharing and seasonal communal feasting as a means of reciprocity and economic redistribution. The rich share time, culture, and emotions as they feed those less fortunate in shared cultural events. The Igbo symbolism of the kola nut, for example, emphasizes the lesson that wealth must be shared by everyone in the community, including the deities and the departed ancestors. Every visit, ceremony, and ritual in the home begins with an invocation and prayer with a kola nut. A piece of kola nut is then placed on the ground for the departed ancestors before the rest is shared. The same procedure is followed on public occasions. In interreligious dialogue the Christian ritual of communion and the Islamic *zakat* are practices comparable to the African tradition of communal sharing.[9] In instances of male monopoly on sharing and blessing, the nurturing power and role of women in African communal feasting provides a good lesson. The positive relational matriarchal African tradition is relevant in interreligious dialogue that critiques the global political economy. Such traditions contradict the theory of neoliberalism, which places private interest above social interest.

Conclusion

International corporations and financial agencies are spearheading the new global economy informed by neoliberalism. They speak the pure profit-oriented language of budget management and growth accounting and force their liberalizing measures on developing countries. There is little concern about the negative social consequences of this sole focus on growth to the exclusion of local social development, an area of major concern to women in Africa.

World Bank policies have been devastating for the poor, and for African women in particular. The cyclical debt that never ends has broken the autonomy and effectiveness of the state in Africa because money that would be used for national development is diverted to servicing the national debt. Debts have not diminished; instead new loans are promised at high interest rates. The promises of SAPs have not been realized. Investment and savings rates are still low. There is no improved export performance, because food export is at the expense of local needs. There is increased unemployment and no evidence of sustained growth. The poor are poorer and suffer the added burden of HIV/AIDS, while the majority of African women are locked in a cycle of poverty.

[9] The *zakat* is a "wealth tax" (stipulated regular charity that demands the distribution of a stated percentage of a fixed amount of property such as cattle, agricultural produce, gold, silver, and merchandise) imposed on the rich to be given to the beggar and the destitute as one of the five pillars of Islam.

I have placed these issues within a gender-informed dialogue about gods and goddesses in a paradigmatic contest of truths, a dialogue with historical and interreligious consequences for our experiences and understanding of greed, civility, rights, social justice, and happiness in local and global contexts. This essay raises theoretical and methodological questions about the study of the religions in Africa and, hopefully, contributes to new perspectives on gender that can enable us to capture more fully the cultural and social dynamism involved in religious beliefs, local economies, and the global political economy.

The salvation of humankind and the harsh reality of global poverty are mutually exclusive. Faith-based groups who speak against international poverty, debt issues, and human rights abuses must do so in the spirit of social justice and not see it as an opportunity to proselytize their faith and convert new followers. A focus on justice will require cooperation with other religions, human rights organizations, and rights workers. Academics and intellectuals also have an important role in the struggle for justice. With a vigorous application of gender analysis, existing data can certainly be challenged to yield new models of social interaction with far-reaching implications for social morals, ethics of human rights, and social justice. The understanding of women's cultures and women's knowledge within local cultures and societies offers important sources of alternative views, even as they critique the political and philosophical concepts of globalization.

Discussion Questions

1. What are the concerns of women in Africa related to development? Compare the traditional Igbo relational matriarchal model and general African thinking about greed and the logic of neoliberalism governing the new global economy.

2. To what extent can Igbo traditions be said to be favorable to women and the idea of an inclusive community in comparison to other traditions discussed in this book?

3. In Igbo and African traditions, a matriarchal religion permeates the entire culture, encourages economic success, reciprocity, and the redistribution of wealth for the general good of the

community. Therefore, the affliction of poverty is not a condition for salvation. Discuss.

SUGGESTED FURTHER READING

Amadiume, Ifi. *Daughters of the Goddess, Daughters of Imperialism: African Women, Culture, Power and Democracy*. London: Zed Books, 2000.

Emecheta, Buchi. *The Joys of Motherhood*. London and Portsmouth, N.H.: Heinemann, 1979.

———. *Kehinde*. London and Portsmouth, N.H.: Heinemann, 1994.

Kaplan, Flora, ed. *Queens, Queen Mothers, Priestesses and Power: Case Studies in African Gender*. New York: New York Academy of Sciences, 1997.

Nwapa, Flora. *Efuru*. London: Heinemann, 1966.

Snyder, Margaret C., and Mary Tadesse. *African Women and Development: A History*. Johannesburg: Witwatersrand University Press; London: Zed Books, 1995.

Chapter 2

Religious Conscience and the Global Economy: An Eastern Perspective on Sociospiritual Activism

By Swami Agnivesh

Abstract

During a period when there is a growing maldistribution of resources around the world and an increase in materialism and desire for acquisitions, Hindus are not the only religious peoples to see a need to activate a religious conscience that has a global dimension to it. However, religions frequently do not avail themselves of their potential to transform societies and reform systems. Instead, the institutionalization of religions often perpetuates the dominant—and frequently wealth-oriented—interests of the day.

It is incumbent upon us to recognize our universal kinship and global responsibilities despite obstacles such as secularism, interfaith disarray, ideologies of greed, a world of gross inequalities, and the atrophy of a sense of community. The Vedic faith, which teaches that the whole of creation derives from God and that we are all one family, seeks to liberate human beings and to pave the way for the emergence of a noble society.

The development of a genuine religious conscience will bring with it a commitment to justice and compassion and it will require greater ethical vigilance and activism in the global community. To transcend greed, we must change our focus from the current emphasis on "having" to "being." Lust for material acquisitions can and must be tempered with love for our fellow human beings, and our accountability to God must increase. This means that our sense of global responsibility must become far more comprehensive than that which we presently see.

All that is there in the universe belongs to God,
Enjoy it sacrificially, Greed not
After all whose wealth is it?[1]

Introduction

The history of the material evolution of our world comprises at least three recognizable stages. From living in a multipolar

[1] This is the first mantra in the last and fortieth chapter of *Yajur Veda* and also the first mantra of *Isa Upanishad.*

world, the human species moved into a bipolar world, especially in the twentieth century. Since the disintegration of the erstwhile Union of Soviet Socialist Republics (USSR), this bipolar world has given way to a unipolar world, a process that is at the core of the emergence of the current world order.[2]

The moral evolution of our species involves a journey in the opposite direction. Morally we begin with a unipolar world: the exclusive preoccupation with the self. We evolve from unipolarity to bipolarity: the willingness to harmonize the instincts of the self with the interests of others. Individuals and groups are poised between this moral unipolarity and bipolarity. That is to say, we can function in terms of exclusive self-absorption, or we can live in a state of dynamic equilibrium: the equilibrium between the self and others. The balance between the self and the non-self comprises the dynamics of ethics. From this perspective, greed is a state of imbalance, the tyranny of unilateralism.[3] It upsets the balance of interests in favor of the self, endangering the health and wholeness of the larger context and, eventually, undermining the foundation for one's own dignity and fulfillment. Violence, both implicit and explicit, is basic to the outlook of greed. In the very nature of things, violence directed against others eventually turns into violence turned against oneself, in ways subtle and broad.

We are in a state of ongoing dialogue with the world around us. Marx posits economic, social, and cultural determinism and allows for a preponderance of material conditions in this dialogue.

[2] Editors' note: Swami Agnivesh makes use of the following terminology, which, in other disciplines, may convey meanings that are different from those intended here: unipolar, bipolar, multipolar.

[3] According to the Vedic *Varnashram Dharma*, in the first stage of a person's evolution (*Brahmacharya Ashram*, the life of a student, which lasts up to approximately twenty-four years of age) a person remains more or less unipolar in his/her way of life. In the next stage, which is *Grihastha Ashram* and spans a person's married life lasting up to the age of fifty, s/he becomes bipolar in nature. In the third phase, namely *Vanaprastha Ashram*, which is a period of growing involvement in social concerns and identification with the community and lasts up to around seventy-five years of age, s/he becomes multipolar. Finally, in *Sanyasa Ashram*, the person transcends all polarities and attains a state of oneness with the Ultimate Reality (*Paramathman*).

And this existential dialogue is woven into the warp and woof of our life. Its shaping influence is steady and deep, the more powerful for our being unaware of it. Spiritually, the boundaries between economics and ethics, creed and culture, remain fluid. Human nature shapes, and is in turn shaped by, culture. This reality makes engaging the present topic something more than an academic luxury. The escalating unipolarity of the global order cannot but have its moral implications, not merely in the form of placing the resources of the world in the hands of fewer and fewer people but also in undermining the ethical equilibrium of our nature at all levels. The economic prospect for unprecedented acquisition could be reinforced by the ethical collapse into an unprecedented lust for acquisitions. Growth and greed could vitiate each other and degrade wealth into a denial of welfare. And the rich, not less than the poor, could be caught in this moral "debt-trap." If the dynamic of global economics becomes unipolar, can ethical dynamics be far behind?

ACTIVATING A RELIGIOUS CONSCIENCE

From a Hindu as well as from an ecumenical perspective, there is a need to activate a religious conscience at the global level. In doing so, there is a need to come to terms with some serious impediments. Hinduism, like all other religions, is not partial or committed to any particular economic or cultural model. From the religious standpoint, whatever is man-made has the potential for good and for evil. The ethical task, from a Hindu perspective, is to enable and enlarge the potential for good and to minimize the scope for evil and exploitation.

When a system reveals itself as consistently defiant and averse to the calls of justice and equality, it creates the rationale for its own annulment. The religious task then is not to prolong its terminal illness but to organize a prompt burial so as to pave the way for the emergence of something new and better. This is the prophetic task that denounces the status quo and announces the new dawn almost in the same breath. According to the *Gita*, even as the forces of evil and injustice mount, a retributive and redemptive intervention on the part of the divine in the form of an avatar takes place.[4] This results in the elimination of the *adharmic* "unrighteous" and the re-establishment of the *dharmic* order, which refers to the right balance emanating from the dharma.[5] Swami Dayanand (1824-1883), the founder of the Arya Samaj, however, takes a distinct and different stand on this issue. He insists that rather than wait for an apocalyptic denouement to historical realities, human beings as agents of moral action are to take on the task of upholding the righteous order.

Borrowing some metaphors from Jesus of Nazareth, one might say that religions of the world have immense potential to be "the salt of the earth and the light of the world." They are meant to value-nourish the world and to safeguard the sanity of our species and the salubrity of creation. But the distressing fact, all through history, is that somehow it has been easier to bring the negative and destructive potential of religions into play in public life than their resources for transforming societies and reforming systems. The fault is not in religions per se; it is in the institutionalization of religion and its subsequent deployment for the defense and perpetuation of the dominant interests of the day. This has given birth to various ideologies and systems of legitimization, draped at times in the swaddling clothes of scripture or tradition. The scope of our theme calls for a quick reckoning of this reality.

The ground reality is that, as of today, we are far away from being a "genuine global order."[6] What has emerged so far is an early model, an edited version, and bias underlies all edited versions of reality. While the current world order is global in some respects, it refuses to be global in many others. It is global in those respects that are beneficial to the industrially advanced nations of

[4] The *Gita* is a sacred Hindu text that takes the form of a philosophical dialogue in which Krishna instructs the prince Arjuna in ethical matters and the nature of God. In Hinduism, "avatar" is the incarnation of a deity in human or animal form to counteract an evil in the world.

[5] In Hinduism, the "dharma" refers to the religious and moral law governing individual and group conduct.

[6] It may be noted in this context that the sixth principle of Arya Samaj is, "The service of the entire world is its primary objective, which includes the physical, social, and spiritual well-being of all."

the world. So trade barriers must go and markets must become accessible globally. But the resource barriers must not go. We are miles away from the mindset of universal kinship and global responsibilities. The walls of ethnocentrism, made thicker through colonialism and the rise of the technological culture, continue to loom large. So the architects and protagonists of the current world order are not perturbed by the fact that twenty percent of the world's population monopolize eighty percent of the earth's resources.

Some of the roadblocks to the emergence of a genuine global order, as well as a shared religious conscience, are listed here.

Secularism

By privatizing religions and exiling them from public space, secularism, for all its many other virtues, paved the way for the hegemony of economics and politics and for the unscrupulous pursuits of both. While religions continued to be practiced in the private domain, religious conscience ceased to be a formative principle in human affairs, locally and nationally. This subverted the cause of social justice, especially in societies without welfare states. Religions continue to be professed, but life as a whole is lived on the foundation of culture, with its preferred models of economics, politics, and science. As long as this outlook remains, the prospect of tempering predatory greed with the sensitivities of a religious conscience remains bleak.

The Interfaith Disarray

A conflicting model of interfaith relationships is the rationale for secularism in a multireligious world. Disunity and competition render religions vulnerable to the seductions of fundamentalism and communalism. In practical terms, what perpetuates these aberrations is human greed. Neither fundamentalism nor communalism is faithful to the true genius of the religion to which they claim allegiance. They are, in one way or another, the cloaks of legitimacy thrown over the nakedness of collective greed. What often drives political ambition, especially in India, is the prospect of unlimited and unethical accumulation of wealth at the expense of the welfare of the people. Communalism seeks to bargain and secure the maximum advantage for a religious community. Religious fundamentalism is a reaction to the threat of change that endangers entrenched political and economic interests. The division of people along religious lines has been the strategy of preference for the protagonists of the status quo in every society. A religious consciousness effective at the global level can be fostered only through a genuine well-directed interreligious movement.

Ideologies of Greed

Greed is integral to the hegemonic spirit of the dominant elite in religion and politics. It seeks to exclude as many people as possible from sharing the fruits of development. This is possible only if they are frozen in underdevelopment and their identity is socially redefined to deny them the right to share the resources available. This involves ascribing different scales of values and different sets of rights to people. Religious texts, often in gross misinterpretation, are deployed to legitimize this injustice. The Hindu *Laws of Manu,* for example, prescribe that the Varna system is based on one's talent, action, and aptitude, not on birth. The elite Brahmin priest-craft upended this scheme of things and evolved a birth-based and oppressive caste system to advance their class interests and to keep the majority of the people outside the zone of sharing resources. This amounted to the worst form of socioeconomic colonization, in the name of religion. The religions of the world have a regrettable track record of having lent themselves to legitimizing and perpetuating the greed of the dominant classes and castes all over the world. Unless this tendency is faced squarely and corrected, the development of a shared religious conscience in combating global greed will remain an ever-receding dream.

A World of Gross Inequalities

The one generalization that we can safely make is that whatever is put in place will be taken over by the dominant interests in that context, irrespective of the founding intention. In the non-Western world we are daily nagged by the anxiety that the current global order is being exploited by the developed societies in the global village. If that is so, the greed of global players could increasingly drive this gigantic system. The comparative vulnerability of non-Western societies makes it nearly impossible to resist these tidal waves of organized greed. It is all the more necessary, therefore, to answer the call of resistance to this aspect of globalization from within the Euro-American bloc. This is possible and feasible only as a spiritual initiative that harnesses the religious resources of the world to imbue the giant of world order with a heart of flesh.

The Atrophy of a Sense of Community

The predatory instinct of humanity, at the micro and macro levels, is checked by a sense of kinship. The role of religion is to hold together, or to reinforce, a sense of kinship, as is evident from its genius to build community. Kinship is the quintessential religious element. The Vedas teach that the whole of creation, including the human family, originates with God. The Bible lays special emphasis on the universal kinship of all human beings by emphasizing that the entire human family is created by God and descended from the same source, Adam and Eve. Similar insights exist in other religions as well. This universal brotherhood is not, however, a manifest reality, but a hidden truth. Geographical, emotional, and cultural distances serve to mask the oneness of the human species. Ideologies of alienation further aggravate our spiritual blindness. The operation of greed, barring exceptions, presupposes alienation. If the neighbor is loved as one loves oneself, there is a good chance that he will be safe from the menace of our greed.

The true Vedic faith is a universally valid and inspiring vision for the liberation of human beings, paving the way for the emergence of a noble society.[7] However, the rise of negative secularism,

[7] The Vedic ideal of *Vasudhaiva Kutumbakam*, which sees the whole of the human species as an extended family, insists on prioritizing the needs of the poor and the powerless. This presupposes a culture of compassion, which today is being swamped by the rising waves of organized greed. The task of subverting greed needs, hence, to be seen as a spiritual enterprise that aims at fostering a global conscience of compassion and social justice.

which denigrated the relevance of religion and the rise of materialistic culture, characterized as it is by profit-driven multiple conflicts, has taken a heavy toll on Hinduism. The rise of Hindu fundamentalism has led to the violation of every dharmic principle upheld by the Vedas.[8] A shrewd use of the media and a variety of mass-mobilization techniques as well as the aggressive selling of a fundamentalist propaganda threaten to spread confusion and cynicism in the minds of the people on the desirability of religion itself. The religious goal envisaged in Hinduism is to help a person move from being an *alpatman*, a person led by his mean or low self, to a *mahatman*, a noble and righteous person. The mix-up between communal politics and politicized Hinduism has already had quite the contrary effect. Today Hinduism is in peril, but not on account of a threat from any other religion. The danger to its authenticity comes from its self-appointed protagonists and promoters.

As we moved from an agrarian to a cosmopolitan culture, our sense of belonging together became progressively diluted. Meanwhile, economic and political institutions began to be more and more gigantic, aggravating the insignificance and virtual invisibility of the human person. This human loss on account of urbanization and industrialization has only worsened in the wake of globalization. In the global order, the agents of greed are no longer national but multinational, a fact that makes them all the more irresistible and intractable. In addition, the victims of organized greed today are not only individuals, but also societies and nations. This has aggravated human helplessness and insignificance to an unprecedented level.

Religious conscience stands in danger of atrophying as we move away incrementally from the individual or the immediate human context. Distance is a poor catalyst for compassion. Human suffering at a distance could easily degenerate into food for sentimentality at best, or mere media fare, at worst. If the religious task in the global arena is confined to making pious pontifications and stirring speeches from international podiums, it is

[8] The term *Veda* refers to any one of a group of sacred hymns and verses composed around 1200 B.C.E. that extol Hindu deities.

unlikely to conjure up a religious consciousness. Religious conscience is much more than mere awareness. It is awareness with a duty to respond. It is knowledge enlivened by justice and compassion. It is knowledge conjoined with the dynamism of love.

THE GLOBAL ORDER

Subverting greed is a perennial need in every organized way of life, because greed is a basic ingredient in human nature. In the global economy, the monster of greed threatens to enjoy a longer leash and farther reach. This calls for greater ethical vigilance and activism in the global community. We need to take several issues into account.

The Autonomy of Economic Processes

In the context of democratic nation-states, economic policies and priorities were reflections of the will of the people. This is almost a thing of the past at the present time. States have become far more responsive to the will of international financial institutions. This amounts to a withering away of the dynamics of democracy. The irony is that such a state of affairs is being conjured up globally by those very centers of power that, until the collapse of the Soviet Union, used to swear by democracy. It is worthwhile, in this context, to remember Professor Amartya Sen's pioneering work in establishing the correlation between democracy and the avoidance of famine and large-scale deprivation in India. The electoral compulsions of democracy used to force the hands of the Indian political establishment to maintain a semblance of balance between greed and need in the culture of governance. The advent of globalization has already upset this balance.

The Wasting of the State

It is logically impossible for a world order to develop and become operative without diluting the authority, compromising the autonomy, and narrowing the jurisdiction of nation-states. Domestically this is marked by the conjunction of globalization and privatization. Internationally this is announced by the combination of globalization, liberalization, and the regulatory regimes that modulate the global economy, such as the International Monetary Fund (IMF), World Bank (WB), and the World Trade Organization (WTO). Liberalization opens the floodgates to multinational corporations (MNCs) that are powerful enough to twist the arms of governments in the developing countries. These transnational pressures are irresistibly powerful, utterly beyond the reach of public opinion and people's resistance at the local and national levels. The MNCs are able to manipulate the market forces and influence domestic economic and industrial policies to maximize their profits. In that sense, globalization has unleashed the dogs of greed in the poorer societies of the world.

The Disempowerment of the Local Community

The contrived euphoria about the global village and global neighborhood masks the sad reality that this is bad news for the cohesion and dynamism of the local community. The more local forms of governance and checks and balances are eroded, the more it escalates the helplessness of the people. Gandhiji's's[9] call for boycotting imported goods points to the pattern of resistance that is still theoretically possible for the victims of globalization. But this may not be as effective now, for several reasons. First, insofar as the national governments are in league with the global players, the ferment of patriotism will not be enunciated in this form of resistance. Second, the power of advertisement has made the masses internalize the seductions of consumerism. Third, the culture of indulgence that has arrived in the wake of globalization has eroded the spirit of resistance.

The Shift from People to Profit

Arguably the most disconcerting feature of the emerging global worldview is the shift from people to profit. This shift has paved the way for subordinating the welfare of the people to the idoliza-

[9] Gandhiji is a nickname for Mohandas K. Gandhi (1869–1948), whose nonviolent resistance led to Indian independence from British rule. M. K. Gandhi is more commonly called Mahatma Gandhi.

tion of profit and the legitimization of greed. This is taking place within a universal "casino culture," with its cult of spinning money out of money and bypassing the ethics and spirituality of work and fulfillment. With this, the shift from rational and work-based expectation to speculation is almost complete. Through organized and remote-controlled manipulation of stocks and money markets in a variety of ways, wealth is made to flee from one hand to the other, and from one society to another. In this way, both the stock market and international banking serve as catalysts of megagreed. Why European banks should enable corrupt Third-World politicians and bureaucrats to stash away the wealth of their respective economies in anonymous overseas accounts, bleeding to death the economies of the poorer peoples of the world, is a question that continues to puzzle the rest of us. From the Afro-Asian perspective, the glitter of European prosperity is tainted by the blood money that sustains this affluence and is wholly disproportionate both to the natural resources and to the economic activity of some of the countries in this region. Though this is not a phenomenon hatched within globalization, it certainly is a scandal that needs to be addressed in the global arena if the oceanic avenues for the practice of greed are to be circumscribed.

The religious mission in such a context is to enunciate and popularize a counter-culture to the emerging and reigning culture of consumerism and indulgence. It calls for a spiritually informed critique of lifestyles so as to keep the focus on justice, equity, and the feeling of fellowship. The Hindu way of life answers the call of this mission by expressly forbidding thriving at the expense either of one's fellow human beings or of other creatures. It sees the integrity of creation as founded on the interdependence of all parts of creation, and, as such, Hinduism rejects the "homo-sapiens-centered" worldview. The Vedas, in fact, state, *"Mata bhoomih, putroham prithivyah,"* which means, "Earth is our mother and we are all her children." The Vedas go so far as to disallow private ownership and the accumulation of earth's resources and urge their collective ownership and equitable sharing. As long as greed continues to be glorified, implicitly or explicitly, and as long as this rising materialistic dogma is not interrogated, the task of subverting greed will not even begin.

Some Moral Issues

The flip side of greed is the callousness and allergy to the poor that it breeds. Institutionalized and implicitly legitimized greed creates a climate of opinion in which human worth is measured in terms of "having" rather than of "being." The only relevant thing about the poor is that they are the "have-nots." That also means that they are a burden on the society, a stumbling block on the path of national progress and prosperity. Until the advent of globalization, poverty was the most important electoral issue in India. Politicians at least paid lip service to the poor and subscribed to the view that those in governance had a duty to ameliorate the suffering of the poor and recognize their aspirations. This ideological element evaporated from the Indian political horizon more quickly than anyone could imagine.

Another key moral issue pertains to technology, because the global order is driven by technology. This fact carries with it a touch of destiny. All of us have internalized it as an inexorable fact that there is no alternative to technology. We are also aware at the same time that technology is not developmentally neutral. It offers advantages to the developed and richer nations of the world, to the greater disadvantage of their poorer brethren in the global village. Technology, historically speaking, is an inextricable part of a mindset and culture of control and manipulation. Technology today adds teeth to human greed to an extent it never did before. Modern technology is qualitatively different from its earlier counterparts.

The absence of affirmative action is yet another moral issue. In a context of gross inequalities accumulated over a period of time there is a need to maintain a margin for reverse discrimination so that equality of opportunity will become a reality rather than remain a teasing illusion. To impose uniform requirements in a state of gross inequality is to aggravate inequality. While the idea of affirmative action has, through a period of prolonged struggle, written itself into the national cultures of governance, the same is conspicuous by its absence in the global arena.

The fueling of corruption is yet another aspect of globalization. Contrary to what was widely expected, the ground reality in many of the Afro-Asian societies is that the proximity of the global neighborhood has fueled rather than contained the forest fires of corruption. The primary reason for this is not hard to identify. Corruption in all societies all too often originates with the ruling elite. Globalization has exposed the elite in all societies to the inflated incomes and lifestyles of affluent societies. Given the outlook of materialism that measures human worth by possession and consumption, it is only natural that the covetousness of the elite in underdeveloped countries went berserk in an effort to catch up with their counterparts elsewhere. The megascams and financial scandals that have rocked India since 1992, when this country launched itself into the orbit of globalization, prove this point convincingly.

The second reason for this flare-up of corruption is that the climate of liberalization and privatization has activated individual greed. The volume of money involved in sleaze operations at present is so huge that it has virtually crippled the arm of law. It may be relevant to note in passing that the extent of corruption that prevailed in Afro-Asian nations was a fairly well-known fact. Yet large sums of monies were advanced as loans by financial institutions, knowing that this would, most likely, end up in anonymous overseas accounts. The amount of money stashed away in foreign banks by Indian politicians and bureaucrats is estimated to be between $100 and $250 billion. It was this that crippled India economically, precipitating an economic crisis that played a big role in forcing this country to fall in line with the globalization process. (International aid, it seems, has plunged us into AIDS of the economic variety!) It is intriguing, for instance, that the IMF imposes strict restrictions on us vis-à-vis subsidies that benefit the poor, but the same institution is totally indifferent to, or is permissive of, corruption that benefits the elite and burdens the poor. For example, there is no ceiling on defense spending, an area where gigantic greed runs amok today. These are blatant instances of legitimizing and enabling greed.

THE DYNAMICS OF RELIGIOUS CONSCIENCE

There are two radically different approaches to dealing with the issue of human greed. The first is to put in place checks and balances so that the predatory and exploitative instincts in human nature do not become socially subversive. This approach is centered in law, complemented by the ideologies and proprieties that prevail in the given context. The main thrust in this approach is to contain the outward expressions of greed and not to root out greed from human nature, which is assumed to be an unattainable ideal. The second approach, however, rejects this assumption and assumes that the persistence of greed and its power over individuals and societies stems from a materialistic worldview. If lust for material acquisitions can be tempered with love for one's fellow human beings and accountability to God, it becomes possible to deal with the problem of greed effectively.[10]

The problem is that the secular-materialistic discourse is resistant to the paradigm shift required in this instance. It is basic to the dogmatism of secular materialism that issues be handled only according to its own premises and resources. We must understand that evolving a religious conscience is a radical task that cannot remain anchored in secular dogmatism. Rather, it must come to terms with the dynamics of an altered paradigm of reality. From such an outlook the radical thing to do is not to "subvert greed" but to promote a spirit of caring and sharing. It is fostering a culture of universal responsibility, responsible stewardship of earth's resources and a sense of global kinship that discourages thriving at the expense of one's fellow human beings as an ugly and undesirable agenda.

In other words, a religious conscience cannot be conjured up in a secular climate of opinion without interrogating the basic assumptions and advocacies and advancing an alternate set of perspectives and goals. A few representative instances will bring clarity to this point.

The Idea of Creation

In the religious worldview, creation is seen as created by God and owned by God. This rules out exclusive human ownership

[10] The Vedas say, "*Shat hast samahra, sahasra hast sankira,*" which means, "Earn with a hundred, but give away with a thousand, hands."

and puts the focus on human stewardship. The idea of stewardship integrates growth with sharing. Hoarding is seen as a defiance and negation of God's ownership. Material goods and fruits of development become the means through which our love for God and our fellow human beings is expressed. By contrast, in the secular outlook, material resources are seen in terms of individual or corporate ownership from which it is difficult to exclude greed.

Our Shared Inheritance

The immediate implication of the insight that God is the primary owner of earth's resources is that earth begins to be seen as the common inheritance of the human species as a whole. In the milieu of the nation-states, it was sufficient to see national resources as a shared heritage for the citizens of a particular country. But genuine global thinking demands that we see the resources of the world as linked to the needs of the people of this planet as a whole. Greed is not only a matter of making excessive or even illicit profits. It is a matter of monopolizing resources far in excess of one's own needs in a world where the basic needs of millions are not met.

Individual Identity vs. Global Family

The religious conscience presupposes a distinctive idea of the individual, his significance, and his social identity. In this vision, the whole of our species is seen as comprising one vast global family. In the Vedas this glorious insight is developed as *vasudhaiva kudumbhakom*, which can be translated as "the whole world is one family." The deep sense of kinship born out of this spiritual insight makes us the keepers and defenders of one another's welfare. Inferentially, it disallows thriving at the expense of others. This has immense potential to keep greed under check.

A Caring Culture

Based on the above, and in recognition of our kinship that interweaves individuals and issues addressed, the genuine religious vision fosters a caring culture. The cornerstone of this culture is the discovery that the inhabitants of this planet are not aliens, strangers, or enemies. Neighbors must inhabit the global neighborhood. This rules out all ideologies and institutions of exclusion and exploitation, such as caste and race. Notions of cultural and religious superiority or inferiority and the imperialistic duties born out of them to help masses migrate from one constituency to the other begin to look naïve and ridiculous in such a light.

While love of material possession drives the culture of greed, the caring culture is driven by love for our fellow human beings. It is in the nature of love to care and to share, and share, if need be, sacrificially. It is at this point that religious conscience begins to frontally engage the crucial question of lifestyles. We cannot maintain a wasteful and indulgent lifestyle and yet remain caring in our outlook. The practical truth is that nobody has enough resources with which to care for anybody else, after all his many and ever-multiplying cravings are satisfied. The sea has limits, says an ancient aphorism, but human desire has none.

This is an issue of special significance, especially for the affluent societies of the world. One explanation of the emergence of the global economic order resonates with the overtone that it was created to buttress the inflated and unsustainable lifestyles of the privileged peoples of the world at the expense of their poorer brethren in the Two-Thirds world. If there is even an iota of truth in this apprehension, the inference becomes irresistible that a conspiracy of organized greed underlies the mantra of market economy.

The challenge is to bring the idea of a caring culture from the haven of pious sentiments to the realm of working realities. This means two things. First, it calls for a change in outlook from wants to needs. Gandhi used to say that this world has enough resources to meet human need, but not enough to meet human greed. Intercultural communication is fostering a move away from need to the gratification of all sorts of wants and desires that continue to multiply in this age of advertisement and hardsell. The more a culture gets obsessed with the gratification of engorged human desires, the more blind it becomes to human needs. Greed, in other words, is incompatible with a caring culture.

Second, the global scenario has to be envisaged in terms of

global responsibility. We in the developed countries are still far from thinking of the world as a whole. Our planet continues to be a theater of competing and conflicting interests. A more comprehensive idea of responsibility is essential to create a caring culture in our global community.

It is important to make practical and institutional provisions that can help realize this changed outlook. It is significant that we have a World Trade Organization (WTO), but no World Stewardship Organization (WSO). This, in itself, points to the order of our priorities. Trade is the god of the marketplace. We need to think of a pro-active Global Economy Court (GEC) or Global Resources Court (GRC) to adjudicate the issues pertaining to the imbalance between the generation of wealth and human welfare on this planet. As of today there is no statutory mandate to ensure a need-based distribution of the resources of the world and to engage the practicalities of affirmative action in the global arena. Above all, a determined effort needs to be made to humanize free enterprise so that it does not degenerate into profiteering even as it remains oriented to profit. Profiteering, unlike the generation of profit, involves a depraved attitude to one's fellow human beings on account of the idolatry of wealth.

At the core of the religious conscience is the spiritual insight that the whole world is one family: *vasudhaiva kudumbhakom*. The idea of "family" embodies the quintessential caring culture. In a family, where love functions, resources are biased in favor of the weak and the handicapped, and not in favor of the able and the privileged. Materialism, unlike love, creates a world order of organized lovelessness that erodes the caring culture.

Subvert or Transcend?

It is doubtful that greed can be "subverted." However, it can be transcended. It is not helpful or sensible to target greed in isolation from the total orientation of the life and culture that prevails. All through the spiritual history of humanity it has been clear that greed is inherent in a mercenary or self-serving way of life, whereas the missionary or other-serving way of life is intended to ennoble and integrate individuals with their neighbors and thereby create caring communities. The worry is that what underlies the current global worldview is a self-serving rather than an other-serving outlook; it is the latter outlook that has the potential for being the purest and most dynamic outward expression of a caring culture based on the religious element of universal kinship. A life dedicated to serving others breaks all human barriers and systems in expressing the justice, compassion, and concerns of God. It insists on a preferential option for the underprivileged, seeing the whole of humankind as an extended family.

In the end, greed is not the primary reality. It is an absence, rather than a presence, like a hole in a sock. The epidemic of greed has to be managed proactively. The religions of the world are based on the belief that it is more blessed to give than to receive. God is seen universally as the Eternal Giver. In Indian thought, the outlook of generosity, with its delight in giving, is considered the essence of peace or *shanti*. Greed is a symptom of our spiritual underdevelopment; it is the outworking of a blindness to the larger and eternal realities of life and destiny. It points to the collapse of our social imagination, which makes us think that cutting the branch on which we are sitting is a profitable activity. The religious vision is that people all over the world together comprise the human family, and one person or society cannot thrive at the expense of another. Our global village, from this perspective, will remain a theater of poverty and underdevelopment as long as there is even a single member of the human family who starves and is denied the right to develop and find fulfillment on this planet of plenty.

It is not for want of good intentions alone that greed continues to engulf the world. The situation is going from bad to worse mainly because a motive for transcending greed and the empowerment to do so are not a felt reality in this world. Acquisitiveness is basic to human nature in a secular-industrial-consumerist way of life. From a spiritual perspective, the realization of God rather than material acquisition is the ultimate goal of life. Unlike in the classic Hindu Vedantist tradition that assumes the material world to be *Maya* or "unreal," the Hindu Vedic tradition recognizes matter as the necessary medium for the soul to attain the Ultimate Bliss, which is God. The insight that excessive attachment to the things of this world is a spiritual snare has been a realization common to all spiritual traditions in the world. The more we are alienated from God, the greater becomes the psychological compulsion to fill this gaping vacuum with the volume of our desire for acquisitions. We turn material possession, without even knowing it, into the fundamental principle of life. Only within a paradigm shift from a wealth-centered to a God-centered way of life does the goal of transcending greed become feasible.

It was from this spiritual perspective that the saints and seers of India evolved the *varnashrma dharma* model of life. In this model, every stage of human life is structured on the principle of transcendence. The key assumption here is that *aparigraha,* "non-acquisitiveness," is central to a dharmic or righteous life. *Varna* is derived from the root *VRI-VRINOTE,* which means "to choose." Here the choice is not of material avenues, but of a mission in life. Every individual soul is called upon in the early stage of one's formation to choose one of the three missions: the mission to overcome ignorance, the mission to overcome injustice, or the mission to overcome inadequacy. A person's vocation is dedicated to the realization of this mission. From a self-centered, mercenary outlook, the individual is gradually led to a humanity-centered, other-oriented outlook. The ownership of the material world rests solely with God, whereas human beings are its collective custodians. As mentioned above, this questions radically the understanding of the private ownership of property and the means of production as absolute goods, which includes the notion that I can acquire as many of the goods of this earth as I want and do whatever I want with them because they are mine. Such a notion of ownership, not only according to Marx but also according to the religions, is the root cause of both inequality and escalating greed.

DISCUSSION QUESTIONS

1. Hinduism envisions human beings as living in a process of constant evolution. Describe how that process of evolution relates to social responsibility.

2. Define the term "religious conscience," including an elaboration of at least three aspects of this concept within your definition.

3. What are some of the roadblocks to a global religious conscience and what must change in order for these roadblocks to be removed?

4. What is the difference between "ownership" and "stewardship"? What relevance do these concepts have to economics?

5. What is the difference between "subverting greed" and "transcending greed" according to Swami Agnivesh's perspective?

SUGGESTED FURTHER READINGS

Chapple, Christopher Key. "Hindu Environmentalism." In *Worldviews and Ecology: Religion, Philosophy, and the Environment,* ed. Mary Evelyn Tucker and John Grim. Maryknoll, N.Y.: Orbis Books, 1994, pp. 113-23.

D'Sa, Francis X. "Lokasanghraha: The Welfare of the Whole World: A Hindu Vision of a World Order." *Jnanadeepa: Pune Journal of Religious Studies* 2 (1999): 47-59.

Painadath, Sebastian. "Mukti: The Hindu Notion of Liberation." In *World Religions and Human Liberation,* ed. Dan Cohn-Sherbok. Maryknoll, N.Y.: Orbis Books, 1992, pp. 63-77.

Tochia, Adila DiUbaldo. "Mahatma Gandhi's 'Real Economics.'" *Religious Studies and Theology* 13/14 (1995): 78-88.

Wilfred, Felix, ed. *Leave the Temple: Indian Paths to Human Liberation.* Maryknoll, N.Y.: Orbis Books, 1992.

Chapter 3

Pave the Planet or Wear Shoes? A Buddhist Perspective on Greed and Globalization

By David R. Loy

Abstract

The goal of the Buddhist path is to end our dissatisfaction with life by "waking up." This does not mean giving up material possessions, but it requires a non-attached attitude toward them. *Dana* ("generosity") is very important as a way of developing our non-attachment as well as helping others. Buddhism does not recommend any particular economic system, although it does emphasize that economic issues are also ethical or spiritual ones. The crucial question is whether an economic system is conducive to the ethical and spiritual development of its members. Does it institutionalize the "three poisons" (greed, ill will, delusion), or does it encourage us to transform them into generosity, loving-kindness, and wisdom? The "engine" of economic globalization is the desire for continual profits and the need to keep people always wanting more; ironically, this does not seem to be making us any happier. Economic theory assumes that resources are limited, but our desires are infinitely expandable. Without self-limitation, this is a formula for strife, since frustrated desires are a major cause of ill will. From a Buddhist perspective capitalism is neither natural nor inevitable, but one historically conditioned way of living that tends to desacralize the earth by commodifying it into resources.

Buddhist Teachings on Wealth and Poverty

Why is Buddhism known as the Middle Way? Shakyamuni Buddha renounced a privileged life of pleasure and leisure for the arduous life of a forest dweller, but ascetic practices did not produce the enlightenment he sought. The middle way he discovered does not simply split the difference between sense-enjoyment and sense-denial. It focuses on calming and understanding the mind, for such insight is what can liberate us from our usual preoccupation with trying to become happy by satisfying our cravings. The goal is not to eradicate all desires, but to experience them in a non-attached way, so we are not controlled by them. Contrary to the stereotype of Buddhism as a world-denying religion, that goal does not necessarily involve transcending this world in order to experience some other one. It means attaining a wisdom that realizes the true nature of this world, including the true nature of oneself.[1]

These concerns are reflected in the Buddhist attitude toward wealth and poverty:

> To know the *dhamma,* to see things truly, is to recognize the self as a conditioned, temporal reality and to reject self-indulgent cravings as harmful illusions. Thus, a non-attached orientation toward life does not require a flat renunciation of all material possessions. Rather, it specifies an attitude to be cultivated and expressed in whatever material condition one finds oneself. To be non-attached is to possess and use material things but not to be possessed or used by them. Therefore, the idea of non-attachment applies all across Buddhist society, to laymen and monk alike. (Sizemore and Swearer 1990, 2).

The main issue is not how poor or wealthy we are, but how we respond to our situation. The wisdom that develops naturally from non-attachment is knowing how to be content with what we have. *Santutthi paramam dhanam,* "the greatest wealth is contentment" (*Dhammapada* 204).

This does not mean that Buddhism encourages poverty or denigrates wealth. As Shakyamuni emphasized many times, the goal of the Buddhist path is to end our *dukkha* (often translated as

[1] As it has spread and adapted to different cultures, Buddhism has changed so much that it is difficult to generalize about its teachings. In this short essay, however, there is no space to distinguish between the different Buddhist traditions. My focus is on the teachings of Shakyamuni as preserved in the Theravada Buddhism of South and Southeast Asia. The Pali sutras, which are believed to record his original teachings, provide a foundation generally accepted by all Buddhist traditions. The Nikayas cited in my text are an important part of those teachings. The *Dhammapada* is a very popular collection of Buddhist aphorisms taken from the Pali canon. In a few places I refer to the teachings of Mahayana Buddhism, which today are found predominantly in North and East Asia.

"suffering" but better understood as "ill-being" or "dissatisfaction"). He summarized his teachings into four noble (or ennobling) truths: life is *dukkha*; the cause of *dukkha* is *tanha,* "craving"; there is an end to *dukkha* (*nirvana*); the way to end *dukkha* is to follow *magga*, "the eightfold path." None of these truths implies material poverty, for poverty is a source of unhappiness in itself and also makes it more difficult to follow a spiritual path.[2] In the *Anguttara Nikaya,* for example, the Buddha says that a life of poverty (*daliddiya*) is miserable, because it leads to (among other things) borrowing, mounting debts, and ever-increasing suffering (III, 350-52).

Shakyamuni also said that there are three types of people in the world. Some are blind in both eyes, because they know neither how to be successful in the world nor how to live a virtuous life; some are blind in one eye, because they know how to pursue worldly success but do not know how to live virtuously; and a few are not blind at all, because they know how to do both (*Anguttara Nikaya* I, 128). As this implies, Buddhism recommends neither material nor moral deprivation.

Nevertheless, it would be a big mistake to conclude that Buddhism approves of a life devoted to acquiring wealth. The ultimate goal of liberating insight may be more difficult to pursue if we are destitute, but a life focused on money may be as bad, or worse. Shakyamuni warned repeatedly against that danger: "Those people who, having obtained vast wealth, are not intoxicated by it, are not led into heedlessness and reckless indulgence which endangers others, are very rare in this world" (*Samyutta Nikaya* I, 74). An intense drive to acquire material riches is one of the main causes of our *dukkha.* It involves much anxiety but very little real satisfaction.

Instead, the Buddha praised those who renounce all attachment to material things in favor of a life devoted wholeheartedly to the path of liberation, by joining the *sangha* community of *bhikkhu* monks and *bhikkhuni* nuns. The minimal needs of such renunciates are known as the four requisites: food sufficient to alleviate hunger and maintain one's health, clothing sufficient to

[2] For example, see the story of the poor peasant in *Digha Nikaya* III, 189-92.

be socially decent and protect the body, shelter sufficient for cultivating the mind, and health care sufficient to cure and prevent illness. Needless to say, this is hardly a recommendation of wealth.

On the other side, however, and despite all the counsel about not being attached to riches, Buddhism does not claim that wealth is in itself an obstacle to following the spiritual path. The five basic precepts that all Buddhists are expected to follow—to avoid killing, stealing, lying, sexual misconduct, and intoxicating drugs—mention nothing about abstaining from wealth or property, although they do imply much about how we should pursue them. The value of money cannot be compared with the supreme goal of enlightenment, yet wealth properly acquired has traditionally been seen as a sign of virtue, and properly used can be a boon for everyone, because wealth creates opportunities to benefit people and to cultivate non-attachment by developing one's generosity. The problem with wealth is not its possession but its abuse. "Wealth destroys the foolish, though not those who search for the goal" (*Dhammapada* 355). In short, what is blameworthy is to earn wealth improperly, to become attached to it and not to spend it for the well-being of everyone, to squander it foolishly or use it to cause suffering to others.[3] Right livelihood, the fifth part of the eightfold path, emphasizes that our work should not harm other living beings and specifically prohibits trading in weapons, poisons, intoxicants, or slaves.

That wealth can indicate virtue follows from the traditional Buddhist belief in karma and rebirth. If karma is an exceptionless law of the universe, what happens to us later (in this life or in a future lifetime) is a result of what we have done in the past and are doing now. This makes one's wealth a consequence of one's own previous generosity, and poverty a result of misbehavior (most likely avarice or seeking wealth in an immoral way). Not all contemporary Buddhists accept that karma is so inexorable, or understand it so literally, but this traditional belief implies our personal responsibility for whatever happens to us and (in the long run, at least) complete harmony between our morality and

[3] See, for example, *Anguttara Nikaya* IV, 285 and II, 67-68; *Samyutta Nikaya* I, 90.

our prosperity. Today, however, the effects of economic globalization and a concern for social justice cast a somewhat different light on this issue. We shall return to this later.

BUDDHIST ECONOMICS

Everything mentioned above concerns attitudes that we as individuals should cultivate or avoid. What kind of economic system do they imply? Buddhism, like Christianity, lacks an intrinsic social theory. The Buddha never taught about economics in the sense that we understand it now. This means that we cannot look to traditional Buddhist texts for specific answers to the economic issues that concern us today. However, some Pali sutras do have significant social implications. Perhaps the most important is the Lion's Roar Sutra (*Cakkavatti-sihanada Sutra*), which shows how poverty can lead to social deterioration.

In this sutra the Buddha tells the story of a monarch in the distant past who initially relied upon the Buddhist teachings, doing as his sage advised: "Let no crime prevail in your kingdom, and to those who are in need, give property." Later, however, he began to rule according to his own ideas and did not give property to the needy. As a result, poverty became widespread. Because of poverty, one man took what was not given (i.e., stole) and was arrested. When the king asked him why he stole, the man said he had nothing to live on. So the king gave him enough property to carry on a business and support his family.

Exactly the same thing happened with another poor man, and when other people heard about this they, too, decided to steal so they would be treated in a similar way. This made the king realize that if he continued to give property to thieves, theft would increase. So he decided to get tough on the next one: "I had better make an end of him, finish him off once for all, and cut his head off." And he did.

At this point in the story we might expect a parable about the importance of deterring crime, but it turns in the opposite direction:

> Hearing about this, people thought: "Now let us get sharp swords made for us, and then we can take from anybody

> what is not given, we will make an end of them, finish them off once and for all and cut off their heads." So, having procured some sharp swords, they launched murderous assaults on villages, towns and cities, and went in for highway-robbery, killing their victims by cutting off their heads.
>
> Thus, from the not giving of property to the needy, poverty became widespread, from the growth of poverty, the taking of what was not given increased, from the increase of theft, the use of weapons increased, from the increased use of weapons, the taking of life increased. . . . (*Digha-Nikaya* III, 65ff., in *The Long Discourses* 396-405)

The long-term result was degradation of life and social collapse.

Despite some fanciful elements, this myth has clear economic implications. Poverty is presented as a root cause of immoral behavior such as theft and violence. The Buddhist solution to such deprivation is not accepting one's "poverty karma." The problem begins when the king neglects his responsibility to give property to those who need it. This influential sutra implies that social breakdown cannot be separated from broader questions about the benevolence of the social order. The solution to poverty-induced crime is not severe punishment but helping people provide for their basic needs.

However, notice also what the sutra does *not* say. Today we usually evaluate such situations by talking about the need for "social justice" and the state's role in "distributive justice." This emphasis on social justice, so central in the Abrahamic religions (Judaism, Christianity, and Islam), is not found in traditional Buddhism. As the above story indicates, this does not mean that Buddhism is insensitive to the problem of poverty, but emphasis on karma implies a different way of understanding and addressing that social problem. The traditional Buddhist solution to poverty is *dana,* "giving" or "generosity."

Dana is the most important concept in Buddhist thinking about society and economics, because it is the main way our nonattachment is cultivated and demonstrated. We are called upon to show compassion to those who need our help. Although the doctrine of karma implies that such unfortunates are reaping the fruit of their previous deeds, this is not understood in a punitive way. They are simply victims of their own ignorance, and the importance of generosity for those walking the Buddhist path does not permit us to be indifferent to their misfortune. We are expected, even spiritually required, to lend what assistance we can. This appeal is not to justice for a victim of circumstances; it is the morality and spiritual progress of the giver that is the issue. In the language of contemporary ethical theory, this is a "virtue ethics." It offers a different perspective that cuts through the usual political opposition between conservative (right) and liberal (left) economic views. According to Buddhism, no one can evade responsibility for one's own deeds and efforts, but generosity is not optional: we have a *spiritual obligation* to respond compassionately to those in need. In the Lion's Roar Sutra, the king started the social breakdown when he did not fulfill this obligation.

Does this emphasis on *dana* offer a viable alternative to modern discourse about social justice? However valuable individual generosity may be as a personal trait, it is difficult to see how that alone could be an adequate response to the widespread social problems being created by rapid economic globalization. It is also difficult for many Buddhists today to accept that increasing poverty, apparently caused by impersonal economic developments, is really just an effect of individual bad karma created in previous lifetimes. The concept of social justice may not be original to Buddhism but neither is it incompatible with Buddhist teachings. Today some socially engaged Buddhists are attempting to incorporate such a concern for social justice into the way they live their faith.

In modern times, the social consequences of *dana* in most Asian Buddhist countries have become somewhat limited because the popular emphasis has been on "making merit" by supporting the *sangha* community of renunciate monks and nuns. The *sangha* is dependent on that support because monks and nuns are not allowed to work for money. Karma is often understood in a commodified way, as something that can be accumulated by *dana*, "giving." Since the amount of merit gained is believed to depend not only upon the value of the gift but also upon the worthiness of the recipient, and since members of the Buddhist *sangha* are viewed as the most worthy recipients, one receives more merit from donating food to a well-fed *bhikkhu* than to a poor and hungry layperson.

This preoccupation with accumulating merit (usually for a better rebirth) may be incompatible with the Buddhist emphasis on non-attachment, as it seems to encourage a "spiritual materialism" that is ultimately at odds with the highest goal of spiritual liberation. However, the benefits of such merit-making rebound on the rest of society, since the *sangha* is primarily responsible for practicing and propagating the teachings of Buddhism. Nevertheless, I believe that the present economic relationship between *sangha* and laypeople needs to be re-examined. Rural Thailand, for example, needs hospitals and clinics more than it needs new temples. According to the popular view, however, a wealthy person gains more merit by funding the construction of a temple—whether or not one already exists in that area. Such a narrow but commonplace understanding of *dana* as merit-making has worked well to provide for *sangha* needs, but cannot be an adequate spiritual response to the challenges provided by globalization.

One possible Buddhist alternative, or supplement, is the *bodhisattva* ideal emphasized in Mahayana Buddhism. The bodhisattva is a spiritually advanced person wholly devoted to responding to the needs of all living beings, not just those of the *sangha.* A bodhisattva's entire life is *dana,* not as a way to accumulate merit but because of the bodhisattva's insight that s/he is not separate from others. According to the usual understanding, a bodhisattva does not follow the eightfold path but a slightly different version that emphasizes perfecting six virtues: *dana*, "generosity," *sila,* "morality," *ksanti,* "patience," *virya,* "vigor," *dhyana,* "meditation," and *prajna,* "wisdom." *Dana,* the first virtue, is believed to imply all the others.

Of course, such a religious model is not easily institutionalized. But that is not the main point. Although *dana* cannot substitute for social justice, there is also no substitute for the social practice of *dana* as a fundamental aspect of any healthy society. When those who have much feel no responsibility for those who have nothing, a social crisis is inevitable.

A Buddhist View of Globalization

We have already noticed that traditional Buddhist teachings do not include a developed social theory yet do have many important social implications. Those implications can be developed to understand and help us respond to the new world order being created by economic globalization.

The first thing to be noticed is also perhaps the most important: As the parable of the unwise king shows, Buddhism does not separate economic issues from ethical or spiritual ones. The notion that economics is a "social science"—discovering and applying impersonal economic laws—obscures two important truths. First, who gets what, and who does not, always has moral dimensions, so production and distribution of economic goods and services should not be left only to the supposedly objective rules of the marketplace. If some people have much more than they need, and many others have much less than they need, some sort of redistribution is necessary. *Dana* is the traditional Buddhist way of redistributing.

The second important truth is that no economic system is value-free; every system of production and consumption encourages the development of certain values and discourages others. As Phra Payutto, Thailand's most distinguished scholar-monk, puts it:

> It may be asked how it is possible for economics to be free of values when, in fact, it is rooted in the human mind. The economic process begins with want, continues with choice, and ends with satisfaction, all of which are functions of the mind. Abstract values are thus the beginning, the middle and the end of economics, and so it is impossible for economics to be value-free. Yet as it stands, many economists avoid any consideration of values, ethics, or mental qualities, despite the fact that these will always have a bearing on economic concerns. (Payutto 1994, 27).

This clarifies the basic Buddhist approach. Individual and social values cannot be delinked. The crucial issue is whether our economic system is conducive to the ethical and spiritual development of its members. When we evaluate an economic system, we should consider not only how efficiently it produces and distributes goods, but also its effects on human values and, through them, its larger social effects. The collective values that our economic system encourages should be consistent with the individual Buddhist values that work to reduce our *dukkha.*

Much of the philosophical reflection on economics has focused on whether economic values are rooted in our basic human nature. Those who defend market capitalism argue that its emphasis on competition and personal gain is grounded in the fact that humans are fundamentally self-centered and self-interested. Critics of capitalism argue that our human nature is less selfish, more cooperative, and generous.

Buddhism avoids that debate by taking a different approach. The Buddha emphasized that we all have both unwholesome and wholesome traits (*kusala/akusalamula*). The important issue is the practical matter of how to reduce our unwholesome characteristics and develop the more wholesome ones. This process is symbolized by the lotus flower. Although rooted in the mud and muck at the bottom of a pond, the lotus grows upward to bloom on the surface, representing our potential to purify ourselves.

What are our unwholesome characteristics? They are usually summarized as the "three poisons" or roots of evil: *lobha,* "greed," *dosa,* "ill will," and *moha,* "delusion."[4] The goal of the Buddhist way of life is to eliminate these roots by transforming them into their positive counterparts: greed into generosity (*dana*), ill will into loving-kindness (*metta*), and delusion into wisdom (*prajna*). If collective economic values cannot be separated from personal moral values, we need to ask: which traits are encouraged by our globalizing economic system?

GREED

Greed is an unpopular word both in corporate boardrooms and in economic theory. Economists talk about demand, but their

[4] The familiar Tibetan Buddhist mandala known as the "Wheel of Life" symbolizes the three poisons as a cock (greed), a snake (ill will), and a pig (delusion), interlocked at the center or axle of the wheel, which as a whole represents samsara, this world of *dukkha.*

attempt to be objective and value-neutral does not allow them to evaluate different types of demand. From a Buddhist perspective, however, our capitalist system promotes and even requires greed in two ways: the "engine" of the economic process is the desire for profit, and in order to keep making that profit people must keep wanting to consume more.

Using these forms of greed to motivate people has been extraordinarily successful—depending, of course, on your definition of success. According to the Worldwatch Institute, more goods and services were consumed in the forty years between 1950 and 1990 (measured in constant dollars) than by all the previous generations in human history (Durning 1992, 38). This binge did not occur by itself; it took a lot of encouragement. According to the *United Nations Human Development Report* (*UNHDR*) for 1999, the world spent at least $435 billion the previous year on advertising, not including public relations and marketing. The result is 270 million "global teens" who now inhabit a single pop-culture world, consuming the same designer clothes, music, and soft drinks.

While this growth has given us opportunities that our grandparents never dreamed of, we have also become more sensitive to the negative consequences, including the staggering ecological impact, and the worsening maldistribution of wealth. A child in the developed countries consumes and pollutes thirty to fifty times as much as a poor one in an undeveloped country, according to the same *UNHDR*. Today 1.3 billion people survive on less than a dollar a day, and almost half the world's population live on less than two dollars a day. The 20 percent of people in the richest countries enjoy 86 percent of the world's consumption, the poorest 20 percent only 1.3 percent—a gap that has worsened in the last decade.

But these grim facts about "their" *dukkha* should not keep us from noticing the consequences for "our own" *dukkha*. From a Buddhist perspective, the fundamental problem with consumerism is the delusion that consuming is the way to be happy. If insatiable desires (*tanha*) are the source of the frustration (*dukkha*) that we experience in our daily lives, then such consumption, which distracts us and intoxicates us, is not the solution to our unhappiness but one of its main symptoms. That brings us to the final irony of our addiction to consumption: according to the 1999 *UNHDR*, the percentage of Americans who considered themselves happy peaked in 1957, despite the fact that consumption per person has more than doubled since then. Nevertheless, studies of U.S. households have found that between 1986 and 1994 the amount of money people *think* they need to live happily has doubled. That seems paradoxical, but it is not difficult to explain: once we define ourselves as consumers, we can never have enough. For reasons we never quite understand, consumerism never really gives us what we want from it; it is always the next thing we buy that will satisfy us.

Higher incomes have enabled many people to become more generous, but increased *dana* has not been the main effect because capitalism is based upon a very different principle, that capital should be used to create more capital. Rather than redistributing our wealth, we prefer to invest that wealth as a means to accumulate more and spend more, regardless of whether or not we need more. This way of thinking has become natural for us, but it is uncommon in societies where advertising has not yet conditioned people into believing that happiness is something you can purchase. International development agencies have been slow to realize what anthropologists have long understood, that in traditional cultures, income is not the primary criterion of well-being. Sometimes it is not even a major one, as Delia Paul discovered in Zambia:

> One of the things we found in the village which surprised us was people's idea of well-being and how that related to having money. We talked to a family, asking them to rank everybody in the village from the richest to the poorest and asking them why they would rank somebody as being less well off, and someone as poor. And we found that in the analysis money meant very little to the people. The person who was ranked as poorest in the village was a man who was probably the only person who was receiving a salary. (Chambers 1997, 179)

His review of the relevant anthropological literature led Robert Chambers to conclude: "Income, the reductionist criterion of normal economists, has never, in my experience or in the evidence I have been able to review, been given explicit primacy" (Chambers 1997, 178).

Isn't it a form of cultural imperialism to assume that we in the "developed" world must know more about worldly well-being than "undeveloped" societies do? Our obsession with economic growth seems natural to us because we have forgotten the historicity of the "needs" we now take for granted, and therefore what, for Buddhism, is an essential human attribute if we are to be happy: the importance of self-limitation, which requires some degree of non-attachment. Until they are seduced by the globalizing dream of a technological cornucopia, it does not occur to traditionally "poor" people to become fixated on fantasies about all the things they might have. Their ends are an expression of the means available to them. We project our own values when we assume that they must be unhappy, and that the only way to become happy is to start on the treadmill of a lifestyle increasingly preoccupied with consumption.

All this is expressed best in a Tibetan Buddhist analogy. The world is full of thorns and sharp stones (and now broken glass too). What should we do about this? One solution is to pave over the entire earth, but a simpler alternative is to wear shoes. "Paving the whole planet" is a good metaphor for our collective technological and economic project. Without the wisdom of self-limitation, we will not be satisfied even when we have used up all the earth's resources. The other solution is for our minds to learn how to "wear shoes," so that our collective ends become an expression of the renewable means that the biosphere provides.

Why do we assume that lack of money and consumer goods must be *dukkha*? That brings us to the heart of the matter. Material wealth has become increasingly important in the "developed" world because of our eroding faith in any other possibility of salvation—for example, in heaven with God, or the secular heaven of a worldly utopia. Increasing our standard of living has become so compulsive for so many of us because it serves as a substitute for traditional religious values.

From that perspective, our evangelical efforts to economically "develop" other societies, which cherish their own spiritual values and community traditions, may be viewed as a contemporary form of religious imperialism, a new kind of mission to convert the heathen. Despite their benighted violence, some "Third-World terrorists" may understand this aspect of globalization better than we do.

ILL WILL

Conventional economic theory assumes that material resources are limited, but our desires are infinitely expandable. Without self-limitation, this situation becomes a formula for strife. As we know, desire frustrated is a major cause—perhaps the major cause—of ill will. The Buddha warned against negative feelings such as envy (*issa*) and avarice (*macchariya*).[5] *Issa* becomes intense when certain possessions are enjoyed by some while others have no opportunity to acquire them. *Macchariya* is the selfish enjoyment of goods while greedily guarding them from others. A society in which such psychological tendencies predominate may be materially wealthy but it is spiritually poor.

The most important point, from a Buddhist perspective, is that our economic emphasis on competition, individual gain, and private possession encourages the development of ill will rather than loving-kindness. A society where people do not feel that they benefit from sharing with one another has already begun to break down.

DELUSION

For its proponents, the globalization of market capitalism is a victory for "free trade" over the inefficiency of protectionism and the corruption of special interests. Free trade seems to realize in the economic sphere the supreme value that we place on freedom. It optimizes access to resources and markets. What could be wrong with that?

Quite a bit, if we view free trade from the rather different perspective provided by Buddhism, which can help us to see

[5] See, for example, *Majjhima Nikaya* I, 281-83, II, 247, and III, 204.

presuppositions usually taken for granted. A Buddhist viewpoint suggests that globalizing capitalism is neither natural (as economists, eager to be scientific, would have us believe) nor inevitable; despite its success, it is only one historically conditioned way of understanding and organizing the world.

The critical stage in the development of market capitalism occurred during the Industrial Revolution (1750-1850 in England), when new technologies led to the "liberation" of a critical mass of land, labor, and capital, which became understood in a new way, as commodities to be bought and sold. The world had to be converted into exchangeable "resources" in order for market forces to interact freely and productively. There was nothing inevitable about this commodification. In fact, it was strongly resisted by most people at the time and was successfully implemented only because of strong government support for it.

For those who had capital to invest, the Industrial Revolution was often very profitable, but, for most people, market commodification seems to have been experienced as a tragedy. The earth (which can be considered our mother as well as our home) became commodified into a collection of resources to be exploited. Human life became commodified into labor, or work time, also priced according to supply and demand. Family patrimony, the cherished inheritance preserved for one's descendants, became commodified into capital for investment, a new source of income for an entrepreneurial few. All three became treated as *means* that the new economy used to generate more capital.

From a religious perspective, an alternative way to describe this process is that the world and its beings (including us) became de-sacralized. When things are treated as commodities they lose their spiritual dimension. Today we see biotechnology doing this to the genetic code of life; soon our awe at the mysteries of reproduction will be replaced by the ultimate shopping experience. The developed world is now largely de-sacralized, but this social and economic transformation is far from finished. That is why the International Monetary Fund (IMF) and the World Trade Organization (WTO) have become so important. Their role is to ensure that nothing stands in the way of converting the rest of the earth—the "undeveloped world," to use our revealing term for it—into resources and markets.

This commodified understanding presupposes a sharp duality between humans and the rest of the earth. All value is created by our goals and desires; the rest of the world has no meaning or value except when it serves our purposes. However natural this dualistic understanding now seems to us, Buddhism views it as delusive. There are different accounts of what Buddha experienced when he became enlightened, but they agree that he realized the nondual interdependence of things. The world is a web; nothing has any reality of its own apart from that web, because everything, including us, is dependent on everything else. The Vietnamese Zen master Thich Nhat Hanh has expressed this well:

> If you are a poet, you will see clearly that there is a cloud floating in this sheet of paper. Without a cloud, there will be no rain; without rain, the trees cannot grow, and without trees we cannot make paper. The cloud is essential for the paper to exist. If the cloud is not here, the sheet of paper cannot be here either. . . .
>
> If we look into this sheet of paper even more deeply, we can see the sunshine in it. If the sunshine is not there, the tree cannot grow. In fact, nothing can grow. Even we cannot grow without sunshine. And so, we know that the sunshine is also in this sheet of paper. The paper and the sunshine inter-are. And if we continue to look, we can see the logger who cut the tree and brought it to the mill to be transformed into paper. And we see the wheat. We know that the logger cannot exist without his daily bread, and therefore the wheat that became his bread is also in this sheet of paper. And the logger's father and mother are in it too. . . .
>
> You cannot point out one thing that is not here—time, space, the earth, the rain, the minerals in the soil, the sunshine, the cloud, the river, the heat. . . . As thin as this sheet of paper is, it contains everything in the universe in it. (Hanh 1988, 3-5)

This interdependence challenges our usual sense of separation from the world. The feeling that I am "in here," inside my head behind my eyes, and the world is "out there" is at the root of our *dukkha*, for it alienates us from the world we are "in." The Buddhist path works by helping us to realize our interdependence and nonduality with the world, and to live in accordance with that. This path is incompatible with a consumerist way of understanding that commodifies the earth and reinforces our delusive sense of separation from it and other people.

Socially Engaged Buddhism

It is easy to criticize, of course, and much more difficult to practice what we preach. How well have Buddhist cultures lived up to the values and ideals presented in this chapter?

Historically, the social role of Asian Buddhism has been limited by the subordination of Buddhist institutions to autocratic and usually oppressive rulers. Colonization by European powers created new problems for indigenous Buddhist cultures, but also introduced Western concepts of democracy, human rights, and social justice. The end of colonialism saw the birth of many "engaged Buddhist" movements, such as Sarvodaya Shramandana (a self-help organization working to revitalize villages in Sri Lanka), Buddhadasa Bhikkhu's Suan Mokkh (reforming Buddhism in modern Thailand), the International Network of Engaged Buddhists (based in Thailand, and incorporating many grassroots, volunteer groups devoted to peace work and community development), and several Japanese organizations including Rissho Kosekai and Soka Gakkai. The most prominent figures have been Tenzin Gyatso, the fourteenth Dalai Lama of Tibet (awarded the Nobel Peace Prize in 1989), and Thich Nhat Hanh, the Vietnamese Zen master, poet, and antiwar activist quoted above (nominated by Martin Luther King Jr. for the Nobel Peace Prize).

In recent years socially engaged Buddhism has become a significant presence in the West as well, as seen for example in the Zen Peacemaker Order (based in New York) and the Buddhist Peace Fellowship, an association of over four thousand mostly

American Buddhists committed both to Buddhist practice and social involvement.[6] Some of the people in these organizations are participating in the recent worldwide movement to ensure that economic globalization benefits people rather than transnational corporations. It is too early to know what the impact of such engaged Buddhism will be, but the synthesis of Buddhist practice and social action seems to be a potent one.

Conclusion

Buddhism began with the enlightenment of Shakyamuni Buddha. His "awakening" (the literal meaning of "Buddha") shows us that it is possible to experience the world in a very different way if we transform our greed into generosity, our ill will into loving-kindness, and our delusions into wisdom. From a materialistic perspective, including the "social science" of economics, such religious orientations are superstitious and escapist. From a Buddhist perspective, however, economic growth and consumerism are unsatisfactory alternatives because they evade the basic problem of life by distracting us with symbolic substitutes such as money, status, and power. Similar critiques of idolatry are found in all the great religions, and rampant economic globalization makes that message all the more important today.[7]

Discussion Questions

1. Does Buddhism encourage a life of poverty? Why or why not?
2. What is *dana*? Why is it so important in Buddhism?
3. What are the "three poisons" (also known as the three roots of evil)? What are their economic implications?
4. What is "socially engaged Buddhism"?

[6] Two informative books on socially engaged Buddhism are *Engaged Buddhism: Buddhist Liberation Movements in Asia* (1996) and *Engaged Buddhism in the West* (2000), both edited by Christopher Queen. See the suggested reading below.

[7] I am grateful to Jon Watts and Santikaro Bhikkhu for their comments on an earlier draft of this paper.

Suggested Further Readings

Buddhist Peace Fellowship web page at http://www.bpf.org/index.html.

Coward, Harold, and Dan Maguire, eds., *Visions of a New Earth: Religious Perspectives on Population, Consumption and Ecology.* Albany: State University of New York Press, 1999.

Queen, Christopher S., ed. *Engaged Buddhism in the West.* Boston: Wisdom Publications, 2000.

Queen, Christopher S., and Sallie B. King, eds. *Engaged Buddhism: Buddhist Liberation Movements in Asia.* Albany: State University of New York Press, 1996.

Schumacher, E. F., *Small Is Beautiful: Economics as if People Mattered.* New York: Harper, 1975.

Chapter 4

A Confucian View of the Global Economy

By Zhou Qin

Abstract

With the rapid globalization in the world economy, economic liberalism has been revived by the transnational corporate elite in the past two decades and is now known as neoliberalism. Its globally sweeping scale and irresistible power make it "neo." In comparison to classical liberalism, which persists as liberal in the sense of no controls from government, neoliberalism simply replaces government with powerful financial institutions like the International Monetary Fund (IMF), the World Trade Organization (WTO), the World Bank, and the Inter-American Development Bank. This sounds attractive to those who already have resources and access to the global economy, because the freedom of movement for capital, goods, and services beyond the boundaries of nations implies boundless profits. It also sounds convincing to the audience immersed in individualistic traditions because globalization will "get government off my back." It even sounds desirable to the poor because an unregulated market is the best way to increase wealth, which will ultimately benefit all.

However, to what extent can we believe the promises of neoliberalism? We have already seen mass protests worldwide voicing concerns regarding economic injustice, undemocratic trading systems, and inhumane policies. In this essay, I analyze some ethical issues revealed by the global economy based upon the Chinese experience of the last two decades. Using the experience of China's accession to the WTO, I question the rules of the game and the moral relevancies from a Confucian perspective. To reflect on the inhumane consequences of a global economy, we must replace the godlike rule of the market with faith from our cultural heritages and replace the profit-oriented sentiment with an integrative worldview upon which a global ethics can be established through dialogues among all religious traditions in the world.

Introduction

In his report to the United Nations (UN) General Assembly in October 1999, UN Secretary-General Kofi Annan described globalization as "an irreversible process, not an option" (Annan 1999). This strong statement reflected an underlying debate that has drawn attention from all directions in the last two decades. On the one hand, globalization of the economy has brought tremendous economic growth and benefits not only to developed countries such as the United States and the members of the European Union, but also to many former Communist satellites such as China and East Germany. On the other hand, however, the number of people living in absolute poverty has, according to the UN, increased from about one billion to 1.2 billion since 1995. While the multinational corporations enthusiastically praise the global economy not only for its unprecedented increase in wealth but also for its meeting the common concern for poverty (Dollar and Kraay 2000), the mass protests worldwide have voiced more fundamental concerns regarding economic injustice, undemocratic trading systems, and inhumane policies.

How can we integrate these opposing viewpoints and attitudes to arrive at a comprehensive view of the global economy? Is it possible to build a new global economic architecture that deals fairly with the world's wealth? Is it possible to derive a better measure by which the global economy can be judged, not only in terms of material benefits, but also in terms of ethics and spiritual well-being?

In this essay, I shall discuss some of the ethical issues reflected in the global economy and question the rules of the game and their moral relevance from a Confucian perspective. My analysis will largely focus on the Chinese experience of globalization in the last two decades, especially the effort to become part of the World Trade Organization. By illustrating the moral failure of globalization in China as well as in the world, I intend to apply a Confucian view to the search for wealth and profit through which an attempt to pursue a healthier global economy would be hopefully taken into consideration.

The Promises and Perils of Globalization in China

In the most general sense, *globalized economy* refers to a process by which goods and services move freely within and among nations without intervention from governments. In other words, the basic rule of the global economy is the rule of the free market: competition.

The underlying concept of this economy is not new at all. It can be traced back to the classical liberalism of Adam Smith

(1723-1790), a Scottish economist who published his masterpiece, *An Inquiry into the Nature and Causes of the Wealth of Nations,* in 1776. With an attractive promise to emerging capitalist nations that free trade was the best way for a nation's economy to develop, Smith advocated the abolition of government intervention in economic matters (Smith 1950). This was the origin of economic liberalism. As the essence of modern Western ideology, economic liberalism is based on individualism, which highlights the core values of Western modernization, including individuality, liberty, human rights, freedom, and self-interest. Though the basic notion of economic liberalism served nations well as an effective means for the early development of capitalism, it did not survive disasters such as the Great Depression or the world wars of the twentieth century. The reason for this is that it lacked concern with, as well as capacities for, promoting the common good in a humane way. In the post–World War II era, the belief that the common good should be the concern of communities and advanced by governments became a consensus among the majority of Europeans and North Americans. In this view, it is obvious that economic liberalism was not able to address the common good in a large-scale human society because of its individualistic value system and profit-oriented rationality.

During the last quarter of the twentieth century, with rapid globalization as well as shrinking profit margins within the world economy, economic liberalism has been revived by the transnational corporate elite, and it is now known as neoliberalism. Its sweeping global scale and irresistible power make it "neo." In comparison with classical liberalism, which is "liberal" in the sense of no controls from government, neoliberalism seeks to replace governments with powerful financial institutions like the International Monetary Fund, the WTO, the World Bank, and the Inter-American Development Bank. This new economic wave sounds attractive, of course, to those who already have resources and means to access the global economy because the total freedom of movement for capital, goods, and services beyond the boundaries of nations implies boundless profits. It also sounds convincing to the audience immersed in individualistic traditions, because the global economy will "get government off my back." It even sounds desirable to the poor or to those concerned with the common good of the community because an unregulated market has been proven to be the best way to increase economic growth and, ultimately, benefit all.

But, to what extent can we believe that this approach (neoliberalism) is the best way to benefit all? Here, I will take one step back and look into the rules of the game in the ongoing global economy as reflected in China's accession to the WTO.

THE WTO AS PARADIGM

The World Trade Organization is an international trade organization consisting of 141 countries (as of May 31, 2001). It is the only global organization dealing with the rules of trade between nations in the world economy. The negotiations for China's accession into the WTO have extended over fifteen years, during which time China has believed that to merge into the global market is the best way to develop its economy. For a process that usually takes one to three years, China's accession to the WTO has become abnormally long. In that time the organization's title has changed from the General Agreement on Tariffs and Trade (GATT) to the WTO, and the U.S. representatives have changed under several administrations. Long Yongtu, the undersecretary of the Ministry of Foreign Trade and Economy, has served as China's chief delegate since 1992, so long that within the talks his name has become a witticism symbolizing the marathon negotiation. In Chinese writing, the character *Long* stands as a dragon that represents the Chinese people, while *Yongtu* literally means endless attempt. Each time the Chinese delegation expects to cross the finish line and reach accord with the global community, it runs into another round of negotiations instead.

One of the major barriers in the WTO negotiations is the liberalization of China's agriculture economy. Although, according to the neoliberals, a globalized market is believed to be the best way to increase economic growth, the starting points in that market are unequal in many ways. The most significant factor is the disparity between countries because of differences in natural resources, development levels, and economic structures. With the largest agricultural population of 900 million peasants and one of the smallest land-to-farmer ratios (at about 0.137 hectare) in the world, China is at a disadvantage. Chinese agriculture will face direct competition with large agribusiness farms in the developed countries which are equipped with larger land-to-farmer ratios (several hundred hectares on average in the U.S., for example), more advanced technology, sufficient capital, and higher government subsidies. In addition to the disparities between countries, there are also disparities between regions within the country and between subsectors within the same sector. China's agricultural conditions in the coastal areas are far more advanced than in the poor inland provinces because of climatic circumstances, technological development, natural resource management, and infrastructure. Also, because of geographical and technological differences, there are labor-intensive sectors producing fruit, vegetables, meat, dairy, and aquatic products, and resource-intensive sectors producing mainly grains and edible oils. Whereas the coastal areas and the labor-intensive sectors are more globally viable in many ways, the inland provinces and resource-intensive sectors are much less flexible to adapt to the demands of a variable global market.

The current conditions for China's competition in globalized agriculture are extremely unequal. Adapting China's agriculture economy to the world market will result in severe upheaval that will harm farm production, income, and employment for millions of people. Even in the long term, the structure of China's agricultural system will not lend itself to a global trading system. As a result, a surge in agricultural goods from farms in the United States and within the European Union (EU) will easily flood China's markets with better-quality and lower-priced produce. This, of course, will benefit urban consumers. However, with an agricultural population of 900 million, the consequences for the peasants will include a sharp increase in poverty and, furthermore, will reduce purchasing power in domestic consumption and financial capacity in investment. Moreover, this flood of affordable foreign produce will also strike at the already low motivation to farm within China and increase the flow of unemployed peasants moving into urban areas, an increasingly serious problem for social stability.

As a result, the globalized trading system magnifies the gaps between developed and the developing countries, coastal regions and inland provinces, and labor-intensive and resource-intensive sectors. These disparities will create further economic inequality as the rich grow richer and the poor grow poorer. When the WTO promises its members a bright future, with very accurate calculations in the growth of wealth, it never reveals the underlying reality that wealth actually shifts under an "invisible hand" from those with fewer resources to those who have more to begin with. In other words, the rules of the game in the global economy help those who are already well-off and damage those who need help to reach the starting line of the race. After all the efforts humankind has made concerning the common good, we now find ourselves stepping back into social Darwinian principles based on life in the jungle—"the survival of the fittest." From the above analysis of China's accession to the WTO, we see a sharp dichotomy between the potential increase in the globalization of wealth and economic injustice at the local, national, and global levels. From this point of view, the promises and perils of globalization in China make it a dangerous game, at best.

A Confucian View of the Rules of the Game

Unquestionably, the basic principle in the global economy is competition—competing freely between nations, regions, firms, and individuals. Historically, the notion of competition has been a key virtue in the West since the beginning of its modernization; indeed, competition has been an essential drive for the growth, development, wealth, and power of the Western nations in their march toward modernity. Epistemologically, this process of progress has formed a strong ideological consensus for the modern West. Competitiveness is not only a great means for an individual to pursue all resources, whether physical, natural, human, or financial, with the greatest possible efficiency; it also serves as a measure for society to judge the success and virtue of an individual. In other words, whoever survives through competition is considered not only a winner but virtuous. Furthermore, competition indicates the core values of individualism in terms of liberty, freedom, individuality, and the pursuit of self-interest by rejecting any restrictions inflicted by familial, social, and political powers. Competition can even make equality possible by imposing the same rules of the game on everyone regardless of social, political, or financial status. In a word, the notion of competition provides a strong rationale for Western modernization that underscores an absolute priority of the individual in human society. However, in spite of its indisputable force and respectable virtue in the rise of the modern West, the dark side of the notion can no longer be ignored.

By highlighting the virtue of competition, neoliberals intentionally neglect the unequal circumstances of human beings throughout the world. Although equality has been conceptualized as a cherished value that upholds each individual's right to be treated equally regardless of origin, race, religion, and social class, human beings are born into inequality in terms of physical genetics, intelligence quotient, gender, family status, etc. It can also be argued that individuals become even more unequal later in life because of social programming, including family circumstances, educational status, and even the environment of one's neighborhood. From this viewpoint, even if one believes in fair and equal competition, the rules of the game are already unequal at the outset.

Confucianism supports a compassionate point of view by seeing each human being as a unique person. Each person comes into life with certain boundaries such as physical condition, family ties, gender, race, historical timing, geographic location, etc. These boundaries also exert an effect on the development of each person. This is an important concept in the Confucian way of maintaining social order, a concept derived from the regulation of nature, namely, *harmony based on diversity*. Only in respecting all differences in myriad things can harmony be obtained. Without difference in tone, there would be no music; in color, no picture; in taste, no delicacies; and in things, no prosperity. This is why Confucius (551-479 B.C.E.), the great teacher of Confucian tradition, advocates, "The gentlemen are harmonious without conformity, and the small men conform without harmony" (*Analects* 13:23). It is clear that the Confucian sense of diversity, as contrasted with the notion of competition, which leads to a tension-oriented society, promotes harmony in the human world.

By acknowledging the differences among human beings in nature, however, Confucianism does not simply support a theory of economic egalitarianism. Rather, it embeds a moral foundation onto the self of each unique person. In Confucian spirituality, the concept of *self* is neither a greedy and hedonistic "self," as we oftentimes celebrate in the West, nor the selflessness of group mentality as understood by some modern minds. The Confucian self is a center of all interactive relations as well as a measure of all things coexisting. On one hand, human beings should never neglect their own needs and interests without which any moral action would lack a point of departure. One should, for example, treat one's parents with more priority than other members in the family, treat other members in the family with more priority than their neighbors, the neighborhood than other parts of the village, the village than the region, the region than the state, the state than other states, and so on. On the other hand, however, self-interest as basic human nature is not merely to generate motivations for individual human beings to pursue their own needs, but also to provide a moral base from which the well-being of others can be considered. When one treats the elders in one's own family with reverence, one will be able to treat similarly the elders in other families; when one treats the young in one's own family with kindness, one will be able to treat similarly the young in other families. This, from the Confucian perspective, is the very essence of moral consciousness. The Confucian self in this context should be understood as a moral agent of a dynamic universe, identified ultimately with a cosmic order by a self-unfolding process, a Confucian "pattern of self-transformation," as Tu Weiming, of Harvard University, would say (Tu 1985, 171-81). This self-unfolding stretches from the near to the far, from oneself to the family, kin, community, state, world, and beyond. Each stage of the process forms a ground to support the one above and provides transcendent forces to penetrate the one below. In this conjunction, the self-interest of each individual should provide a moral ground concerning the needs of others as well as balancing the value of the individual and the value of society.

In light of the teachings of Confucian tradition, neoliberalism and the global economy contribute to the moral disorientation and shallowness of our time. Today, it would be absolutely reasonable for one to claim all of one's rights as an individual without any concerns for the rights of others. To many people who accept this neoliberal philosophy, the miserable circumstances of others are no longer morally disturbing. By virtue of our fundamental commitment to individualism, the underlying ideology to which we are most deeply attracted works on the assumption that the ultimate value of each individual is him/herself. Moreover, the fundamental error of neoliberalism, as well as globalization, lies in supposing that under the justification of unconditional competition, human society can be directed and improved by the rule of the free market alone. In other words, under a seemingly promising theme of rejecting the intervention of government, the market mechanism may be allowed to guide not merely the growth of wealth but the fate of humankind. This view reduces the human world to a big marketplace where everyone is a commercial animal, driven to satisfy all needs by the same sole measure, namely, the power of purchase. One can buy goods, services, entertainment, and even politicians.

ANCIENT WAYS, OLD DREAMS, NEW OPPORTUNITIES

In the case of the global economy in general and the WTO in particular, China's desire to become a member of the world community is a century-old dream of wealth and power in a new global context. Despite the disadvantages outlined earlier, the majority of the Chinese are excited about China's growing participation in the global economy. The domestic level of enthusiasm in this context is abnormally high when one considers the basically unfavorable terms offered to China. The answer to why China is anxious to accept unfavorable trade terms can be found by looking into a century-long self-designated persona with which China has moved toward modernity.

Heshang (Deathsong of the River), one of the most popular TV series in China, was broadcast twice and watched by more than 200 million people in 1988. It narrates the destiny of the Chinese civilization as foreshadowed by a historical event at the dawn of Western modernization (Su and Wang 1991). In the year 1405, a great naval fleet completely unmatched in the fifteenth-century world, riding in the lee of a strong northeast monsoon, grandly set sail from Wuhumen in Fujian. This was the first armada in human history to sail into the Pacific Ocean. Consisting of more than three hundred "treasure ships," some measuring four hundred feet long with crews numbering twenty-eight thousand men, this fleet made seven voyages over the course of twenty-eight years from the China Seas. It crossed the Indian Ocean and reached as far away as Arabia and the east coast of Africa.[1] The purpose of these voyages, however, still puzzles people today. Human history had never before witnessed navigation on such a grand scale yet without an economic purpose. Ironically, this unprecedented navigation took place nearly one hundred years before Columbus sailed west in the so-called Age of Exploration. Zheng He (1371-1435), the commander of the fleet and official of the Ming Dynasty (1368-1644), did not fully appreciate the opportunity offered by primacy on the ocean, an opportunity later to be seized by other civilizations for trade, conquest, and colonization. With a tone of regret, *Heshang* harshly criticizes the land-based fixation of the Chinese civilization as follows:

> Hegel says that the ocean invites mankind to conquest and to trade. And yet the Chinese who answered the invitation of the Pacific were such modest gentlemen who "upheld righteousness and did not scheme for profit" (Ban, Han shu, p. 2524). . . . History chose the Chinese people, but the Chinese people were unable to choose history. Only a few decades later, four small sailing ships under the command of the Portuguese Vasco da Gama (1469-1524), representing an infant capitalism, sailed into the Indian Ocean in search of wealth and markets. By that time, Zheng He's great fleet had already entirely disappeared from the Pacific and Indian Oceans. But it was the Europeans who began the great adventure of geographical exploration. (Su and Wang 1991, 132-33).

Here, we see a sharp divergence within the cultural value systems of the Confucian China and the modern West in approach-

[1] For a more detailed account, see Levathes 1994.

ing wealth. From a Confucian perspective, profit has to give way to righteousness, without which human society cannot be maintained in harmony. This ancient value system seems, however, to have failed its modern transition to a certain extent. While the Chinese and the Europeans dramatically missed each other in the century of exploration, the far-reaching implications of this near-miss were unknown to the Chinese until they were unexpectedly confronted by the offspring of the European explorers nearly five hundred years later with the events triggering the Opium War. This encounter brought China her first taste of tragic defeat on the world stage and, at once, opened a new historical epoch for the Chinese people, an epoch acknowledged later as the beginning of China's transformation toward modernization.

As reflected in *Heshang*, the modern fate of the Chinese civilization was determined long ago, even before the time of Zheng He. Chinese intellectuals place blame for the shrinking back of their great ancient civilization on the traditional Confucian attitude toward profit and competition, namely, placing the priority of morality over the priority of profit and that of harmony over competition. This value system was responsible for China's modern fate because the Chinese were taught to despise material success in social practice and lack aggressiveness in their orientation to life. From this viewpoint, Chinese modernization was relentlessly driven by Western gunboats yet reinforced by its own intellectuals in a process derived from its Confucian past. As announced by the authors of *Heshang* in reflecting on the national experience of Zheng He, the Chinese now strongly assert, "We can no longer afford to lose a single further opportunity offered by fate," and "We will never again turn down the invitation of the ocean!" (Su and Wang 1991, 134). Chinese modernization can be characterized today as a radical mindset of national survival in which the desire to excel in the search for wealth and power is unconditionally highlighted as a dominant ideology born in reaction to a tragic and embarrassing set of historical incidents.

The statement quoted was made in the 1980s, the first decade after the end of Mao's era in 1976. It is worth noting about the 1980s that while the nation was celebrating deviations from Mao's China in all dimensions, there was one direction in which Mao's ideology not only endured, but was propelled further across the country: the radical iconoclasm in the legacy of modern China since the May Fourth Movement of 1919. As reflected in the *Heshang* TV series, the entire nation was deeply in fear of being continuously left behind in modernization, more precisely, in westernization. By characterizing the modern West as an oceanic civilization in comparison to the inland civilization of China, Chinese intellectuals in the 1980s woke up the old nation with a breathtaking slogan, "Embrace the Blueness!" The color blue symbolizes the oceanic civilizations of the West and indicates a total rejection of the traditional Chinese cultural metaphors, such as the Yellow River, Yellow Emperor, Yellow Dragon, Yellow Earth, and even the people with yellow skin. A wholesale endorsement of westernization became an overwhelmingly dominant theme in China. The nation thus awakened and continued her long journey in responding to the invitation of the ocean. Only this time, the invitation was sent by the ocean of profit.

Indisputably, China has achieved incredible economic success in the last two decades. As the fastest-growing economy in the world today, China has raised per capita income to more than four times what it was in 1978. China has also broken records in distributive inequality in the past two decades. The Gini coefficient[2] has, according to the official report from China, increased from 0.28 in the beginning of the 1980s to 0.458 in 2000 (Zhong 2001). Although the calculation methods are debatable, never before has any nation produced such an increasing rate in inequality of wealth distribution in a twenty-year period. Presently, the wealth of the top fifty richest Chinese citizens equals the yearly income of 50 million Chinese peasants; and the wealth of all of the estimated 3 million millionaires[3] in China equals a two-year income for the 900 million peasants in the entire country (Zhong 2001).

[2] A coefficient, based on the Lorenz curve, showing the degree of inequality in a frequency distribution such as personal incomes. The larger the coefficient, the higher the degree of dispersion.

[3] This large number of millionaires is counted in RMB, the Chinese currency, not in American dollars.

The imbalance between economic growth and distributive equality has been a crucial issue for all nations as they modernize. As early as 1959, the UN placed priority on economic growth over justice in developing countries (He 1998). Economic growth often comes at the cost of social injustice, and victimizing behavior is not seen as criminally unjust but as normal and indeed, at times, as virtuous. The ethical issues embedded in China's practice in her economic growth today are fairly compatible with the UN Assembly and not inconsistent with the Western understanding of national economic growth.

In the last two decades of China's economic reform, the conflicts between economic growth and distributive equality have already been brought to light. However, because of the so-called enlightenment mentality, a term introduced by Tu Weiming (Tu 1994), the ethical issue hidden within China's economic growth has rarely been brought forth for discussion. In Chinese modernization since the beginning of the twentieth century, the enlightenment mentality has been a dominant ideology in China's socialist experience as well as in its capitalist experiment. This was especially the case after the Cultural Revolution (1966-1976), when the country opened to economic and political reform.

It is true that when people talk about potential long-term profits of globalization in China, they do acknowledge the short-term damages such as reducing products in agriculture, increasing unemployment, and letting go old, inefficient methods of production. They also promise that these damages will be rewarded soon by the advent of long-term benefits. But few have pointed out the unfair nature of this exchange: investments taken from the problematic companies, laid-off workers, and inland peasants will be the price for providing rewards to the competitive companies, those already well-off, the coastal peasants, and the urban consumers. Moreover, no matter how good the long-term benefits may be, these victims will probably never have a chance to get back to business again because of their disadvantages in competition.

One of the biggest contributors to the rapidly increasing economic disparity in China is unemployment resulting from heavy layoffs in urban areas where big state-owned companies have failed to survive for various reasons. Crouched within the miserable situation of urban unemployment, the hidden ethical issue is this: years of work by thousands of Chinese workers are being transferred into foreign corporate hands. Why should individual workers with a lifetime of contributions to the state-owned companies not take their share of the value to secure their retirement? Why do these workers, after having made all their contributions to the society, deserve to be kicked out in order to give way to a more advanced economy? Why must the economic growth of a nation be built on the victimization of its own citizens, especially the poorer and less capable ones? Under the enlightenment mentality, however, the voice considering these ethical issues of the global economy is hardly to be heard. From a recent report, we read a message from a Chinese official, nomarch of Guangdong province, "We are not afraid of competing (with foreign companies). Whoever cannot survive will be turned into manure in order to make the newcomers stronger" (Chen 2001).

In a Confucian sense, it is shameful if a society leaves its poorer and less capable unprotected. Encouraging the rich and the competent to take unlimited profit based upon the victimization of the former is also shameful. When a society obtains economic benefits based upon the suffering of its own citizens, how can other members of the society be content with these benefits? The consequences of globalization, no matter how greatly they would benefit economic growth, have failed to uphold social justice in consideration of both social harmony and the well-being of the individual. Confucius points out wisely that poverty occurred mainly because of unequal distribution, for where there is equal distribution there is no such thing as poverty (*Analects* 16:1).

Confucian Ethics and the Global Economy

It is not my intention to simply express a negative attitude and protest against the rich or the transnational corporations to illustrate the moral failure of globalization and the burning desire for wealth and power in China. Rather, my intention throughout this essay is to apply a Confucian view of wealth and profit through which the nature of the global economy might be transformed.

Confucianism

It may be a surprise to the majority of Western readers that the Confucian tradition places no less weight than the West does on the value of individual human pursuits, including pursuing personal wealth. Confucius himself said, "If wealth were a permissible pursuit, I would be willing even to act as a guard holding a whip outside the market place" (*Analects* 4:5). Elsewhere, he asserted, "It is a shameful matter to be poor and humble when the Way prevails in the state" (*Analects* 8:13). However, when Confucius talked about being willing to act as a guard holding a whip outside the marketplace in pursuing wealth, he was actually addressing the propriety of the pursuit, the ground on which the legitimacy of personal wealth is rooted.

The concerns of permissibility and propriety in pursuing wealth are based upon a fundamental cosmological worldview in which Confucian ethics is formed. In this worldview, relations between self and the other, the individual and community, the private and public, are not dichotomous but coexistent within a dynamic cosmological setting. The self, the individual, and the private are encompassed in embodying the universe from near to far; whereas the other, the community, and the public are inclusive in penetrating all under heaven from above to below. When compared with a family, the person is the self, individual and private; compared with a community, the family is the self, individual and private; compared with a state, the community is the self, individual and private; compared with the globe, the state is the self, individual and private; and compared with the universe, the globe is the self, individual and private. It is not difficult to see that the communal entities of each level cannot exist without the participation of the individual body below; it is also not difficult to see that the individual beings of each level cannot grow without the nourishment of the communal unit above. On the whole, this cosmological faith in Confucianism is psychologically derived from human sentiment, socially represented in interpersonal relations, politically connected to the propriety of ruling groups, and religiously related to the ultimate commitment that is grounded in the cosmic order. In other words, moral consciousness as a structural thread runs through the sensibility of persons, the mutuality of communities, the legitimacy of authorities, and the religiosity of the civilization.

In light of this anthropocosmic view, permissibility and propriety in pursuing wealth are based not only on considerations of others, but also on matters of self-completion and self-realization. There were two powerful trends in the intellectual discourse during the formation of Confucian ethics, namely, Yang Zhu's egoism and Mo Di's universalism. The former was absorbed in an exclusive self-interested orientation while the latter was totally committed to an impartial universal love. Mencius (371-289 B.C.E.?), one of the most influential disciples of Confucius, described these two trends as follows:

> Yang Zhu's choice was "everyone for himself." Though he might benefit the entire world by plucking out a single hair, he would not do it. Mo Di advocated universal love. If by rubbing smooth his whole body from head to foot he could benefit the world, he would do it. (Mencius 7A: 26)

Despite their fame in the later part of the first millennium B.C.E., neither egoism nor universalism lasted more than a few generations, because the reasoning of their ethics was not rooted in the nature of humans in general and the structure of Chinese culture in particular. These concepts failed to stress the moral responsibility of each person to the community, on the one hand, and to respect the uniqueness of each human being as a moral carrier, on the other. In this famous debate, Mencius brought up a third figure, with which he made an important moral distinction:

> Zi Mo holds the mean between the two, and he is nearer the right. Holding the mean without allowing for special circumstances is like holding on to one particular thing. The reason why I hate holding to one thing is because it destroys the Way. It takes up one point but neglects a hundred others. (Mencius, 7A:26)

The mean between the selfishness of egoism and selflessness of universalism is the ultimate rule of the Confucian Way. The self as the center of all relations and a measure of all things in Confucian ethics differs from egoism and universalism for it is in an open structure in which one extends one's action to others based on one's own interest and understanding of self-realization. The notion *tui*, "to extend," is crucial and unique in Confucian ethics. The egoists respected the self as a center yet failed to extend their action to the other. The universalists, on the contrary, cared for others yet failed to plant the care into the real ground of the individual.

From this Confucian perspective, China must mainly base its search for compatibility and participation in the global economy on its economic and cultural autonomy. This is not only for the sake of its own profit, but also to bring diversity to and share responsibility in building a healthier world economy with all other civilizations. Generally speaking, our world is now characterized by a sharp economic disparity and a great variety in cultures. The rules of the game in globalization are, however, shaped and imposed primarily by the transnational corporate elite of the advanced industrialized countries.

This reality has severely threatened the economic and cultural autonomy of developing countries. In seeking participation in the global economy, for example, China not only offered overwhelmingly favorable concessions in the bilateral talks to the United States and other countries, but also caved in to the rules of the game.[4] Globalization has raised many important issues beyond the economic, of which national and cultural are among the most important. It is truly necessary for China to have better foreign and economic policies as it seeks to take its place in the global forum without selling out to it and, thereby, damaging its own people. For example, China should insist on its position as a developing country in the WTO in order to protect its own

[4] This is particularly true in the issues of protocols. For example, in the case of the MFA (the Multifiber Agreement that restricts textile and garment trade), even after the ten-year phase-out of the MFA proposed by the U.S., quotas could still be imposed on China's textile exports for five additional years. Therefore, in spite of China's strength in garment production, China will not be able to compete freely with other suppliers because of the restrictive quotas in accordance with the MFA. This treatment was even characterized by the U.S. Senator Phil Gramm (Republican, Texas) as "outright discrimination" (Lardy 1999a).

people from unfavorable competition in global trading, especially in the most vulnerable agricultural area. It is more important, however, that China should never give up its own cultural value and Confucian tradition, with which a dynamic interaction among the nations can take place. Only by acting nationally and autonomously can China contribute to a new global economic architecture that deals fairly with the world's wealth and articulates new ethical and spiritual measures by which the global economy can be judged.

The essential teaching that Confucian tradition may offer to the dialogue on globalization can be illustrated in the universal Golden Rule existing in all great traditions: "Do not do unto others what you would not want others to do unto you" (*Analects* 12:2). This principle, as an initial step toward a moral consideration of others, is based upon a self-understanding of one's own interest. Stated in the negative, this principle has, in most cases, to do with self-restriction in taking action that would perhaps benefit oneself but damage the other. Whether or not to impose damage to others in one's search for self-interest is a very basic consideration in human action. Confucius was quite clear about this:

> Wealth and high station are what men desire; but unless I get them in the proper way I would not remain in them. Poverty and low station are what men dislike; but if they can only be avoided to the detriment of the proper way I would accept them. (*Analects* 4:5)

The propriety here is based on a moral consideration of the circumstances of the other resulting from one's action in self-interest. In traditional China, not to take an "improper profit" is not only a rule of social behavior, but also, more importantly, a deep-rooted conviction about respecting the other as coexisting within the same cosmological order as oneself.

Furthermore, the Golden Rule in Confucian tradition is also stated positively: "In order to establish ourselves, we must help others to establish themselves; in order to enlarge ourselves, we have to help others to enlarge themselves" (*Analects* 6:30). This requires further considerations toward human communities at all levels in terms of common interest, mutual benefit, and productive interchange. As we reflect on the inhumane situations in the global economy, we must rely upon our humanity to save ourselves. We must replace the godlike rule of the market with the faith of our cultural heritages, and we must replace the profit-oriented sentiment with an integrative worldview upon which a global ethics can be established through dialogue among all religious traditions in the world. With such a worldview, the "manure" with which we "make newcomers stronger" will be derived from the contributions of individual human beings rooted within the consideration of others in the human world and coexisting altogether with myriad things between heaven and earth.

DISCUSSION QUESTIONS

1. Discuss the dilemma in China's search for wealth and power in its modernization. What is the essential conflict the Chinese intellectuals face between the modern fate of the nation and its Confucian past? How has this either/or choice affected China's attempts to pursue its global compatibility?

2. Analyze the dichotomy between wealth growth and economic injustice in the Chinese experience of globalization.

3. What is the Confucian perspective on the notion of competition? Why can human society not be directed by the rule of the free market alone?

4. Give your suggestions and ideas on an alternative toward a healthier world economy.

SUGGESTED FURTHER READINGS

Confucius. *The Analects (Lun yu).* Translated with an introduction by D. C. Lau. New York: Penguin Books, 1979.

Daedalus (Special Issue Entitled *Multiple Modernities*) 129, no. 1 (Winter 2000).

Mencius. *Mencius.* Translated with an introduction by D. C. Lau. New York: Penguin Books, 1970.

Tu Weiming. "Beyond the Enlightenment Mentality." In *Worldviews and Ecology: Religion, Philosophy, and the Environment,* ed. Mary Evelyn Tucker and John Grim. Maryknoll, N.Y.: Orbis Books, 1994, pp. 19-29.

Chapter 5

Judaism and Economic Reform

By Norman Solomon

Abstract

The present economic order is marred by social and economic injustice among and within nations and the overexploitation and destruction of natural resources. Scripture is not concerned with designing an economic "system," but rather with how to implement justice and compassion within any given system. While Judaism does not identify progress with the increased provision of material goods and services, it does teach us to look after the poor, to heal the sick, to provide food and shelter for those in need, to educate, and to pursue justice. All these injunctions demand material as well as personal resources.

Is it possible to engage in the pursuit of wealth without succumbing to greed and selfishness? Can wealth be distributed equitably? Are citizens of poor countries poor *because of* the present system, or *in spite of* the system?

Implementing Jubilee and Sabbatical years provides a means to address the four major issues which confront us now in dealing with Third-World debt: social injustice in the distribution of wealth, work opportunities, environmental issues, and the stability of population as reflected in the sustained relationship between people and land.

Judaism advocates education toward integrity, honesty, and a work ethic based on responsibility to family, employer, employee, society, and the environment. Wealth is held in trust from God; we are responsible for ensuring its fair distribution.

On Judaism and Economics

The principal sources of Judaism are the Hebrew Scriptures (called the "Old Testament" by Christians) and the Talmud. The Talmud, completed around 600 C.E.,[1] centers on the Mishna, a law code compiled in Palestine c. 210 C.E. The Talmud interprets and supplements the Scriptures, and a large body of literature known as "rabbinic literature" has grown up around both the Bible and the Talmud as they have been interpreted and put into practice in different ages and societies.

[1] C.E., for "current era," is used by Jews in preference to the specifically Christian A.D., which is an abbreviation of the Latin *Anno Domini,* "the year of our Lord."

Since the classical sources of Judaism were compiled many centuries ago, they do not directly address issues of global economics in terms of twenty-first century economic analysis. Nevertheless, they contain much material that can help us formulate a perspective on these issues. How those sources are used, and how their values can be implemented in our global society, are matters of debate; it is important to distinguish which matters can be decided on the basis of the religious sources and which matters depend on a more technical economic analysis for their resolution.

Even on the broadest level it is dangerous to equate biblical provisions with modern economic theories. For instance, in Judaism as in other religions, Scripture has been cited in support of both centrally controlled socialist economies and free-market principles, just as in earlier times it was cited both for and against the institution of slavery. The truth seems to be that Scripture is not concerned with designing an economic "system," but rather with how to implement justice and compassion within any given system.

The sources of Judeo-Christian religious tradition address both ends and means. "Love your neighbor as yourself" (Lev. 19:18) and "Justice, justice shall you pursue" (Deut. 16:20) define the ends or values that ought to guide economic activity; economic activity should be conducted in a manner that (a) shows concern for the well-being of the other and (b) is equitable.[2]

These broad statements of principle are supplemented, in Scripture and the rabbinic tradition, with detailed guidance to just and compassionate personal behavior, together with some indications of the means by which social justice might be implemented in society. This guidance, expressed through the *mitzvot* ("commandments") in the system of *halakha* ("law"), offers a path to attain the objective of creating a just and compassionate society. "Love your neighbor" is supplemented by numerous *mitzvot* and exhortations relating to almsgiving and other forms of indi-

[2] All translations are the author's own except where otherwise indicated. Depending on which version of the Bible you consult, there may be slight variations in the English translations.

vidual and collective benevolence; "pursue justice" is supplemented by a full commercial and criminal code.

Aims and objectives can be formulated at a universal level, and at this level it is easy to see that the biblical objective of creating a just and compassionate society is still relevant. Laws, however, can only be formulated with a specific society in mind. We must ask whether and to what extent it is possible to build on the laws formulated by the Bible and the rabbis in our undertaking to achieve justice and compassion at a global level in the technologically sophisticated, international, and multicultural society of today.

THE PRESENT ECONOMIC ORDER

Religious people do not identify progress with the increased provision of material goods and services. Nevertheless, most religions teach us to look after the poor, to heal the sick, to provide food and shelter for those in need, to educate, and to pursue justice. All of these counsels demand material and personal resources. Even from a religious point of view, therefore, we are justified in regarding the growth of wealth and material resources as a major element in human progress toward the kind of world we believe God wants us to strive for.

Based on this idea that material wealth serves God, the creation of wealth becomes not only acceptable but desirable. However, the desirability of the creation of wealth raises two major issues for religious people. At the individual, personal level, is it possible to engage in the pursuit of wealth without succumbing to greed and selfishness? Second, at all levels of society, right up to the global level, there is the vexing problem of distribution: can wealth be distributed equitably?

For reasons that will become clear, we begin with the second issue. The most obvious success of the present global economic system is its efficiency in the provision of services, the processing of resources, and the production of goods. Only large, transnational enterprises can achieve the levels of investment and economies of scale to do this; only a technology-driven global economy can create a climate for profitable transnational corporations. Even governments, when they fund major defense, education, and welfare projects, are dependent on revenues raised by direct or indirect taxation of such enterprises.

While the global economy maximizes resources and production, the most obvious deficiency of the system is the uneven distribution of wealth. It is, of course, extremely difficult to measure wealth, and even more difficult to measure human happiness. In 1996[3] the United States per capita income was $28,495, and Burkina Faso's was $230. The world average was $5,170. Furthermore, the U.S. figure was increasing, and Burkina Faso's was declining.[4] Citizens of the U.S. may, on average, receive incomes 124 times higher than those of citizens of Burkina Faso, but no one would claim that citizens of the U.S. are, on average, 124 times *happier* than those of Burkina Faso. Moreover, the statistical average conceals unevenness within each country; some citizens of the U.S. are poorer than some citizens of Burkina Faso. Nevertheless, from a religious standpoint, it is grossly unjust that such discrepancies exist.

Are citizens of poor countries poor *because of* the present system, or *in spite of* the system? Were the people of Burkina Faso ever significantly wealthier than they are now? If not, is the cause of their present poverty "the international system" or perhaps local corruption, political instability, or uncontrolled population increase which outstrips productivity? (On the last point, note that the 1996 birthrate/1000 was U.S. 14.9 and Burkina Faso 47, against a world average of 25.)[5]

Whatever the causes of the vast disparities we see, the result of these disparities is social and economic injustice among and within nations and the overexploitation and destruction of natural resources. Third-World debt is one of the most worrying consequences of the economic imbalance that exists, and environmental degradation is another.

[3] Statistics in this section have been taken from the *Encyclopedia Britannica,* DVD edition, 2001.

[4] Statistics compiled about five years previously were U.S. $24,700, Burkina Faso $326, a discrepancy of a mere 76:1.

[5] *Encyclopedia Britannica,* DVD edition, 2001.

TOWARD A JEWISH "ECONOMIC THEORY"

Judaism does not provide a ready-made, comprehensive economic theory, but it does offer guidance on paradigms to those with the technical expertise to construct economic theories. We will first consider attitudes toward wealth, justice, equity, and benevolence. After that, we will inquire what specific biblical legislation can tell us about economic principles, using as our examples the prohibition of charging interest on loans (Exod. 22:24; Lev. 25:36, 37; Deut. 23:20, 21) and the regulations governing the Sabbatical and Jubilee years. Every Sabbatical, or seventh, year, land lay fallow and debts were cancelled (Lev. 25:1-7); every Jubilee, or fiftieth year, slaves were given their freedom and land returned to its owner (Lev. 25:8-55).

Attitudes Toward Wealth and the Pursuit of Wealth

Psalm 24 opens with the words, "The earth is the Lord's and the fullness thereof." In other words, all that we are and all we possess belong absolutely to God. Poverty, the rabbis taught, "is a wheel that rolls around the world."[6] Rags or riches can be anyone's lot, for ownership of material goods is a temporary trusteeship granted by God. It follows from this that ownership is a God-given privilege and carries with it the responsibility of right use.

At Usha in Galilee in the second century the rabbis decreed that no one should give away more than one-fifth of his assets at one time and thus become dependent on others.[7] As Maimonides a thousand years later expressed it, one who brings poverty on himself by dissipating his resources and becoming dependent on others is a fool (Maimonides 8:13).[8] Real poverty is an affliction, not a virtue.

[6] Babylonian Talmud *Shabbat* 151b, attributed to the school of Rabbi Ishmael. See also *Tur: Yore Deah* 247.

[7] Babylonian Talmud *Ketubot* 50a. It is clear from the codes (for instance, *Shulkhan Arukh: Yoreh Deah* 249) that this limit does not apply where the need is great or where one is making a will.

[8] Maimonides, Moses, *Mishneh Torah: Arakhin Vaharamin* 8:13. Significantly, Maimonides codified this rule in the section of his work dealing with temple gifts rather than in the section on charity.

Both riches and poverty challenge a person's moral commitment. The biblical sage Agur bin Jakeh prayed, ". . . give me neither poverty nor riches, provide me only with my daily bread, for if I have plenty I may deny thee and say, 'Who is the Lord?' And if I am reduced to poverty, I may steal and take in vain the name of my God" (Prov. 30:8).[9] Nevertheless, the rabbis condemned the pursuit of wealth for its own sake as a major evil, responsible through envy and greed for human conflict and for turning people away from God.

Jewish moralistic literature discourages individuals from engaging more than absolutely necessary in commerce; one should seek one's basic needs, that is all (*histapkut*). Moshe Hayyim Luzzatto (1707-46) wrote eloquently on this concept:

> For there is no worldly pleasure upon whose heels some sin does not follow. For example, food and drink when free from all dietary prohibitions are permitted, but filling oneself brings in its wake the putting off of the yoke of Heaven, and drinking of wine brings in its wake licentiousness and other varieties of evil. . . . If he is once made to lack his usual fare he will be painfully aware of the fact and will thrust himself into the heat of the race for possessions and property so that his table will be spread in accordance with his desires. He will thence be drawn on to wrongdoing and theft, and thence to taking oaths and to all the other sins that follow in its wake; and he will depart from the Divine service, from Torah and from prayer. . . . (Luzzatto 1987, 183)

A strong tradition, however, endorses the dignity of labor:

> Happy are all who fear the Lord and walk in his ways. When you eat the fruit of your own labor, you shall be happy and it will be good for you. (Ps. 128)

The Bible here portrays the contentment that comes to those who are blessed with self-sufficiency and are free from depen-

[9] This concept is elaborated by the thirteenth-century Spanish Jewish philosopher and exegete Bachya ben Asher in his *Kad Hakemach*. For a translation of the relevant section, see Chavel 1980, 484.

dence on the "gifts of flesh and blood."[10] Ben Zoma, a rabbi of the second century, asked, "Who is rich? He who rejoices in his portion."[11] Ben Zoma knew that one had to have a portion in which to rejoice, and he would have understood well the malaise of the unemployed even where they were not actually suffering extreme deprivation.

Justice and Benevolence

Much *halakha,* or Jewish "religious law," as expressed in codes and in the responsa (written replies to specific questions addressed to rabbis), is devoted to the regulation of commerce, including matters such as just price, competition, and employment. Edward Zipperstein's summary of the twelfth-century *Sefer Hasidim* on employer/employee relations conveys the importance of this matter:

> An employer must not impose superfluous hardship on employees, nor may he demand that the workers exceed their capabilities or strength . . . local custom is a prime consideration in many instances.
>
> Workers must be enabled to come home prior to sunset on the Sabbath and holidays. The pregnant maidservant is to be extended special consideration. . . .
>
> An employer is not permitted to embarrass, insult, belittle or degrade an employee. An employer is not permitted to withhold a worker's pay in order to recover a debt. . . . Promptness of (wage) payment is stressed by Biblical edict (Leviticus 19:13).
>
> Providing employment is a most significant form of benevolence. Placing a person's job in jeopardy is considered an evil act. In hiring an employee, preference is to be granted to the applicant less capable of performing the task, since the more capable person will no doubt be able to obtain employment, but the employment possibilities of the less capable may be questionable.

[10] "Let us not be in need of the gifts of flesh and blood" (fourth paragraph of the Orthodox Jewish grace after meals).

[11] Mishna *Avot* 4:1.

> For compensation (sc. payment) received, the worker is expected to render proper, capable and efficient service to the employer. The employee is not permitted to waste time, slack off in his performance, interrupt his work, leave his work, or engage in unnecessary time-consuming conversations. . . . Jewish law does not favour the protection of any particular group, employer, or employee, rich or poor. Equal rights and justice is demanded from all parties. (Zipperstein 1983, 115)[12]

How can we move from the medieval source summarized by Zipperstein to the realities of contemporary life? For instance, within the framework of the medieval Jewish community it was feasible, when hiring an employee, to grant preference to the less capable applicant. Is this still possible—or even desirable—with today's large, impersonal firms, skill-based efficiency, and widespread unemployment? We might perhaps regard the rule mentioned as a prototype of affirmative action, or of the sort of requirement now mandated in many states that businesses over a certain size must employ a minimum quota of disabled people. Clearly, the application of these early sources in our own society demands careful judgement; the questions remain valid, but the solutions can be controversial.

Public welfare provision is another area for which precedent may be found in *halakha*. But even when we have agreed, in principle, that workers and others should benefit from improved health care and the like, we have to decide whether this should be paid for out of public money (national or local taxes) or private sources (insurance plans paid for by employer, employee, or a combination). There is ample precedent in the responsa and in the *taqqanot* ("local directives") of medieval communities to sup-

[12] Zipperstein is dependent on Abraham Cronbach's article, "Social Thinking in the Sefer Hasidim," *Hebrew Union College Annual* 22 (1949): 1-147. He has, perhaps, misunderstood Cronbach's citation on p. 6 of this article; *Sefer Hasidim* recommends (Parma edition #1020) that preference be given to an applicant who lacks other skills and, hence, has less opportunity for employment, not that preference be given to an applicant "less capable of performing the task" in question.

port the notion that people might be communally taxed for "charity," under which heading most of the money that now goes for welfare would be classified (Freehof 1959, 121-24).

Love and Benevolence

Almsgiving features prominently in Jewish teaching and practice, and the rabbis constantly impressed on their followers the need for compassion and charity. The Hebrew word *tsedaka* ("almsgiving") derives from a root meaning to be "right, fair, or correct." Almsgiving is not so much piety as fairness, ensuring correct distribution of the wealth God has entrusted to us. As we shall see in the following tale, almsgiving is part of *hesed*, which in biblical Hebrew means "love" or "compassion" and is frequently translated "lovingkindness."

The Talmud[13] attributes a discussion on benevolence to the sage Rabbi Akiva and Tinneius Rufus, Roman governor of Judea at the outbreak of the Bar Kokhba War in 132 C.E. The general taunted Akiva, "If your God loves the poor, why does He not support them?" The rabbi replied, "So that through [caring for] them[14] we may be saved from the judgment of hell." The general persisted, "Suppose an earthly king was angry with his servant and put him in prison and ordered that he should be given no food or drink, and a man went and gave him food and drink. If the king heard, would he not be angry with him? And you are called 'servants,' as it is written, *For the children of Israel are my servants*'" (Lev. 25:55). Akiva responded, "Suppose an earthly king was angry with one of his children, and put him in prison and ordered that no food or drink should be given to him, and someone went and gave him food and drink. If the king heard of it, would he not send him a present? And we are called 'children,' as it is written, *You are children of the Lord your God*" (Deut. 14:1).

The late-twentieth-century American rabbi and scholar Isadore Twersky formulated a theory of benevolence on the basis of this story (Twersky 1982, 137). The five points he derives from it are as follows:

[13] Babylonian Talmud *Bava Batra* 10a.

[14] That is, through the virtue of charity.

1. God has, in a manner of speaking, abdicated to His people part of His own function in order to enable them to transcend mere biological existence. When we practice benevolence we share directly in His work.
2. We are all equal, all "children of God"; even our sin and temporary disgrace do not abrogate this relationship.
3. The fact that God's judgment has condemned an individual to poverty does not allow us to sit in judgment on that person or to desist from giving help; his situation challenges us to vigorous ethical response.
4. We cannot "dismiss a destitute person with a counterfeit expression of faith: 'Rely on God . . . ! He will help you.'" We are the ones who must help.
5. *Halakha* (Jewish law, which regulates benevolence) is the system of rules by which a principle of faith is anchored into a detailed ethical code. It encourages spontaneous giving yet provides a discipline which does not leave the poor dependent on the moods and whims of the rich.

The Talmud, like most traditional religious writings, addresses its counsel to the individual, or at most to the community. In modern states, much that in earlier times depended entirely on private benevolence is funded in part or in whole by state taxation. This does not relieve the individual of all responsibility; it enlarges and complicates it. How, for instance, should international aid be channelled? The private individual has a minor role to play in direct assistance, but a more significant role in lobbying governments and large corporations or charities to give appropriate aid.

Interest

The Bible forbids Israelites to charge for lending money or food to fellow Israelites. "If you lend money to any of my people . . . do not be like a creditor, do not impose interest on him" (Exod. 22:24). "If your brother gets poor . . . you shall help him . . . take no interest nor increase from him . . ." (Lev. 25:35-37). "Do not lend on interest to your brother, interest on money or on food . . ." (Deut. 23:20). However, "Lend on interest to a foreigner . . ." (Deut. 23:21).

Psalm 15 and a large part of Ezekiel 18 are lavish in their praise of him "who does not put out his money on usury"; the Talmud glosses, "even to a non-Jew."[15] Economic circumstances, not least the role of Jews as court and church financiers and their exclusion from many "normal" occupations, led Jews in the Middle Ages to revert to the biblical norm of lending on interest to non-Jews.

Moses Maimonides (1138-1204) classified lending, including *ribit* ("interest") among the laws intended to teach compassion (Maimonides 1963, 3:39).[16] Joseph Karo (1475-1588) likewise incorporated the laws of *ribit,* not in the civil and criminal law division of his great law code, the *Shulhan 'Arukh*, but among "religious" laws in the division that contains also the laws of charity.[17] The underlying thought seems to be that the charging of interest, unlike for instance theft, is not an intrinsic moral wrong; the forgoing of interest is more akin to an act of personal benevolence, though unlike a charitable gift it is not optional, at least within the community. The Christian scholastic Albertus Magnus (1200-1280), a teacher of Thomas Aquinas, likewise founded the doctrines of just price and usury on the duty of love.

Modern commerce relies even more heavily than medieval commerce on credit. Jewish law permits borrowing on the basis of a document, the *hetter 'isqa* (analogous to the Islamic *Qirad* and medieval Christian *commendite*), that converts the loan into a business participation in which the lender may suffer loss as well as profit. Since in practice the lender is unlikely to suffer loss, some people view the arrangement as something of a legal fiction, that dresses up one form of transaction as another. But those who defend it argue that the underlying principle that interest may not be taken on a loan, though profit may be made through an investment where there is also risk of loss, has been preserved.

Sabbatical and Jubilee Years

The Jubilee and Sabbatical year regulations in the Code of Holiness (Lev. 25) directly address the issue of the unfair distrib-

[15] Babylonian Talmud *Makkot* 24a. Compare Kimhi's commentary on Psalm 22:23.

[16] See also Babylonian Talmud *Makkot* 24a.

[17] *Shulhan 'Arukh Yore De'ah* 159-77.

ution of wealth. In the seventh year the land "rests" and recovers from its exploitation and debts are remitted; in the fiftieth year, land returns to its hereditary smallholders who, themselves, hold it only on trust from God, and slaves go free. These regulations aim to ensure that wealth is not concentrated in the hands of the few, that families are not uprooted from their patrimony, and that no Israelite is permanently enslaved.

We do not know whether the Levitical regulations were ever fully implemented; perhaps they represent an ideal as yet unfulfilled. It would, in any case, be naïve to apply to the contemporary global situation rules addressed to a particular society in the first millennium B.C.E.; the rules are only fully relevant within the idealized society of Israel as envisaged in Leviticus. Yet with careful, contextual reading, it is possible to infer basic principles on which we can build an approach to modern problems.

Leviticus assumes that population remains stable. If population increases, or even if population increases in some tribal areas and declines in others, the system of land distribution breaks down. On a grand scale, the decline of the Carolingian Empire can be attributed to the simple fact that its founder Charlemagne (742-814) had too many descendants, each of whom claimed an inheritance. Leviticus's idealized picture of parcels of land allotted in the days of Joshua being enjoyed in perpetuity by the families to whom they had been granted depends on each of those families remaining very much the same size in perpetuity—not a likely scenario.

Another assumption is that things will go wrong if left alone. This may be the most important single lesson we can derive from Leviticus. We should always assume that even if we set up the best system of rules we can devise, things *will* go wrong. People will learn to beat the system. They will start to exploit one another, and some will seize the others' territory and amass wealth while others will become poor. So we must frame additional laws to put everything right every now and then, say every seven years, with a major clean-up once in fifty years, like the Sabbatical and Jubilee years.

A third assumption is that slavery will continue to exist, both the enslavement of one Israelite by another and the enslavement of the heathen from the surrounding—or displaced—nations. In this respect at least we have made progress. Pockets of slavery do persist in the world, and we must not close our eyes to them. However, we trivialize the evil of slavery if, like Marx, we refer to underpaid employees as "wage slaves."

Leviticus, in instituting the cancellation of debt at the end of each seven-year period, clearly has in mind accumulated private debt, in an agrarian, pre-industrial society. Is this concept equally applicable to commercial borrowing in a highly developed industrial society or to the international financing of state economies? And if it is not equally applicable, is there perhaps some analogous form of debt remission which could be implemented in certain circumstances? The greatest difficulty to be faced here is not the actual cost of writing off Third-World debt, but the effect this might have on the future availability of credit. Who would lend if they thought the debt might be cancelled? In the too few instances in which an international debt has been written off this problem has been overcome, but only because the special circumstances have been clearly defined.

In sum, the Jubilee and Sabbatical years address the four major issues which confront us now in dealing with Third-World debt: social injustice in the distribution of wealth, work opportunities, environmental issues, and the stability of population as reflected in the sustained relationship between people and land.

CRITIQUE OF THE RELIGIOUS TRADITION

There are three main areas in which the Jewish tradition presents difficulties when we turn to it for guidance in contemporary global economic issues. They are are follows:

- the paradox of self-interest
- the problem of extrapolation
- the need to differentiate between moral and technical issues

The Paradox of Self-Interest

Is it possible to engage in the pursuit of wealth without succumbing to greed and selfishness? In 1776 Adam Smith, in *An Inquiry into the Nature and Causes of the Wealth of Nations*, argued that the pursuit of self-interest, far from undermining the moral fabric of society, as all the religions seem to have taught, actually resulted in the maximization of social well-being. Smith, the classical advocate of laissez-faire economics, also formulated the classical expression (greatly elaborated by later economists) of the need for appropriate government intervention:

> According to the system of natural liberty, the sovereign has only three duties to attend to . . . first, the duty of protecting the society from the violence and invasion of independent societies; secondly, the duty of protecting, as far as possible, every member of the society from the injustice or oppression of every other member of it, or the duty of establishing an exact administration of justice; and, thirdly, the duty of erecting and maintaining certain public works and certain institutions, which it can never be for the interest of any individual, or small number of individuals, to erect and maintain, because the profit could never repay the expense to any individual or small number of individuals, though it may frequently do much more than repay it to a great society. (Smith 1950, II: 184-85)

Smith endorses "the pursuit of self-interest" rather than personal greed, but it is not easy to distinguish between the two, except perhaps with regard to the degree of personal restraint involved. Many of the most successful entrepreneurs, who at some stage in their lives have generously endowed hospitals, schools, improved working conditions, and spearheaded other virtuous projects, were undoubtedly motivated by personal greed and ambition to become rich and famous. This creates what can be called either a paradox or a dilemma: The benefit of the many is secured by the greed of the few.

Perhaps the rabbis were thinking along these lines when they declared that "If not for the evil inclination no one would build a house, marry a wife, beget children or engage in commerce."[18] Likewise, they report that the men of the Great Synod prayed successfully that the temptation of idolatry be abolished. They then prayed for the abolition of lust, and this was granted. But when

[18] Midrash *Genesis Rabbah* 9.

they saw, after three days, that "not an egg was laid in the whole land of Israel" they relented just to the extent that was necessary to ensure human survival.[19]

We must not lightly conclude that because the creation of wealth enhances our ability to do better things for our fellow humans and it is, in itself, a desirable activity, that it does not matter how it is pursued. The end does not justify any and every means by which it may be attained. The religions are in a position to call for ethical standards in commerce. It can be very difficult, however, for an individual in a competitive situation to maintain those standards unless they are sustained by public law. At the global level, such laws have to be secured by international agreements. This is not an easy task since different nations and cultures have different concepts of what constitutes corrupt practice.

The Extrapolation Problem

We have already illustrated the difficulty of applying laws, for instance those on employer/employee relations, in societies vastly different from the one in which the laws were formulated. Even so, the value system on which those laws appear to be based may be refined and developed beyond its original area of application; we illustrated this in the section above on the Sabbatical and Jubilee years.

A further difficulty arises specifically in extrapolating contemporary meaning from the rabbinic sources. Most rabbinic wisdom is couched in terms of "Israel," that is, the Jewish people. Rabbinic hermeneutics restricted the application of some biblical rules to the faithful among the people of Israel. This restrictive interpretation leaves the rabbis with the problem of how to apply such basic ideas as respect for property rights and regard for human dignity to all people, including those outside the Jewish community.

Their solution was to step beyond the system of rules and to formulate a series of broad principles which they used *inter alia* to govern the relationships of Jews to those outside the bond of faith or peoplehood.[20] These principles include the following:

[19] Babylonian Talmud *Yoma* 69b, commenting on Nehemiah 9.

[20] See Ernst Simon's essay "The Neighbour We Shall Love" (Fox 1975, 29-

- *tiqqun olam,* "establishing the world aright"
- *darkei shalom,* "the ways of peace"
- *darkei noam,* "the ways of pleasantness"
- *qiddush Hashem,* "sanctifying God's name," that is, behaving in such a manner as to bring credit to God
- *mishum eiva,* "on account of hatred." This was invoked to justify departure from the standard law in situations where to follow it might stir up enmity between Jews and non-Jews[21]

These aims (fairness, peace, pleasantness, godliness, avoidance of provocation) are vital in setting the agenda for a peaceful world; they convey an overriding moral imperative to seek peace.

However, the simplest approach would seem to be to understand "Israel" in the Bible and rabbinic sources as a paradigm. True, the values of Torah are worked out in terms of Israel, that is Jews, and with a particular society in mind. But this should be understood as an example, to be applied mutatis mutandis to other nations and ultimately to global society. Some *halakha*, such as ritual legislation, is clearly oriented to Israel, though it will have parallels in other cultures. Much is of broader relevance and can be transposed with appropriate changes to other societies. At its heart are truly universal values, and it is these which we must find ways to implement at a global level.

Technical Matters

People would not go to the sources of their religion to discover how to repair their automobile, though they might invoke religion to help them decide whether to drive it to the hospital to

---

56) for an attempt to define the application of the "golden rule" within Judaism. Simon has not clearly grasped the fact that the rabbis used general ethical principles rather than specific scriptural "rules" to regulate behavior toward those "outside the covenant."

[21] *Tiqqun olam* is, strictly speaking, an "extra-legal" measure introduced within the community to avoid impossible situations arising; cf. Babylonian Talmud *Gittin* 34b, 36a. The *locus classicus* for *darkei shalom* is Mishna *Gittin* 5:8-9. *Qiddush Hashem* often bears the meaning of "martyrdom"; for its use in setting standards of moral behavior in dealings with non-Jews, see Babylonian Talmud *Yevamot* 79a; *Bava Qama* 113a.

visit a sick friend or to the casino to gamble. Much the same applies to the global economy. Whether to spend time making money or meditating is a problem somebody might decide by reference to religious values. But how to generate or distribute wealth most efficiently is a technical problem, vastly more complex than how to build an automobile.

Even if you decide to make money you have to make ethical decisions—how to treat your employees, co-directors, and shareholders; what constitutes fair competition or just price; how your activities affect the environment. These decisions will be affected by your religious outlook. But the determination of the most efficient method to manufacture your product, of its potential effects on the environment, of the most effective way to market it, are not primarily determined by ethics, even though ethics may determine whether or not the most efficient method should be used.

This is why so much religious antagonism to multinational companies, or whatever the "bogey" of the moment may be, is injudicious. Multinational corporations as such are not necessarily evil. Perhaps they are the most efficient and environmentally sound means we have to produce and distribute goods and services, or perhaps not, or more likely some are and some are not. But all this must be evaluated in economic, not religious, terms, and only when the economic evaluation has been done can we formulate the ethical questions to which religious considerations may be relevant.

The ethical questions themselves often have to be decided in a political context. International commerce has outdistanced international political cooperation. Multinational corporations are forced to operate under multiple jurisdictions, often without coordinated international regulation. Governments, not companies, carry the ultimate responsibility for protection of the environment and the welfare of their citizens. In this there is hope, for democratic governments are answerable to the people; citizens, religious and otherwise, are able and therefore morally obliged to influence global ethics by lobbying their governments and international institutions.

Conclusion—A Jewish Contribution to the Current Debate

Education

Appropriate education is a priority for any nation to create and sustain the economic base necessary to support what the United Nations' Universal Declaration of Human Rights acknowledges as the legitimate rights of all people, including the rights to life, liberty, and security of person; to freedom from arbitrary arrest; to a fair trial; to be presumed innocent until proved guilty; to freedom from interference with the privacy of one's home and correspondence; to freedom of movement and residence; to asylum, nationality, and ownership of property; to freedom of thought, conscience, religion, opinion, and expression; to association, peaceful assembly, and participation in government; to social security, work, rest, and a standard of living adequate for health and well-being; to education; and to participation in the social life of one's community.[22]

Consideration of this list demonstrates that human rights are expensive; adequate social security, for instance, is problematic even in a wealthy nation like the United Kingdom. Yet much of the money intended by the international community to help less developed nations has in the past served merely to enrich and aggrandize governments, administrators, and middlemen. Corruption may well be the greatest single cause of international funds being locally diverted to ends other than those for which they were loaned. Religion surely has an important part to play in molding public culture to abhor corruption.

Even where there is no corruption, a government has to decide how to allocate its resources. What comes first? How does any government decide how much of its budget to allocate to education, to welfare, or to defense? If such decisions are difficult for rich nations, they are agonizing for poor ones. Poor nations are

[22] Summary of articles 3-27 of the Universal Declaration of Human Rights, adopted as resolution 217 A (III) by the General Assembly of the United Nations on December 10, 1948.

often tempted to cut education since the damage is not immediately apparent; few are physically injured or hungry as a direct effect of lack of education. The damage is indirect and long-term, since the basis for the future success of the individual and the society is eroded.

Two sorts of education are vital for economic success, the technical and the moral/cultural. Technical education includes training in skills appropriate to the technological development and economic resources of the country, as well as management techniques to ensure that the skills are efficiently used in service or manufacture and that the end products are effectively marketed. Moral and cultural education, in which religion plays a part, must cultivate honesty and a work ethic based on a sense of responsibility to family, work associates (employer and employee), society, and the environment.

Religions regard greed, envy, and ambition as vices. However, means must be found to harness these natural tendencies to productivity while moderating their harmful aspects; education, legislation, and leisure pursuits all contribute to the constructive channelling of energy.

Significance of the Jubilee

No permanent remedy is readily available to heal the sickness of poverty and the maldistribution of wealth—"for the poor shall not cease out of the land" (Deut. 15:11). To believe in such a remedy is a utopian fallacy. Much, however, can be and should be done to alleviate hardship both internationally and locally, even if the solutions are partial and impermanent. On this limited basis, "there shall be no poor among you" (Deut. 15:4).

When we enter into the dialogue of Israel with God about people and land, wealth, and poverty, we discover the universal values (justice, love, human equality, and harmony with the land and with God) for which the Torah of ancient Israel is a paradigm that can be applied to our contemporary world. An ongoing dialectic with Scripture as a base—in particular the Sabbatical and Jubilee passages—will provide a fruitful beginning. We must engage in dialogue with economists, sociologists, educators, and experts in natural sciences including environmental studies. This dialogue will help reveal the particular ways in which the "eternal" values can be most effectively pursued in our time. Our approach must never be doctrinaire, but pragmatic, heuristic, with constant feedback and monitoring of the system. We must commit to a readiness to start again if things go wrong, as they certainly will from time to time.

Below is a synopsis of the laws on economic matters in Leviticus. First comes a restatement of each law or group of laws; each restatement is followed by a suggestion of how the law can be extended to become relevant to the needs of contemporary global society.

- Aim at the fair distribution of wealth, work, and credit (numerous laws on care of those in need, and the "marginalized").
  Global extension—let the rich nations assist the poor.
- Provide credit for those who need it, but not in such a way that they cannot discharge their debts (no interest).
  Global extension—international finance, favorable terms.
- Provide opportunity for remission of excessive debt (sabbatical release).
  Global extension—rescheduling and remission of debt.
- Do not overexploit the land (let it "rest" every seven years).
  Global extension—conserve the environment.
- Preserve the bond between people and land (land reverts to original owner in fifty years).
  Global extension—traditional land rights should be respected as far as compatible with economic realities; as fewer people work on the land, our ultimate dependence on its resources and our love for it must find fresh ways of expression.
- The land is held as a trust from God (". . . for the land is mine, and you are strangers and sojourners with me"—Lev. 25:23).
  Global extension—the planet is held as a trust from God.
- Periodically when things go wrong, as they inevitably will in the course of time, joyfully "overhaul" the system (Jubilee "year of freedom").
  Global extension—some will enrich themselves at the expense of

others, some will be placed under the domination of others. Be ready from time to time to make the necessary adjustments to bring freedom to all, in joy, peace, and common humanity.

All this implies a full and active program for the improvement of the world economic order. In sum: The planet is held as a trust from God. Development is subject to the constraints needed to conserve the environment; it must be sustainable over the long term. Our common humanity under God demands that the rich nations assist the poor. International finance must be provided under favorable terms, without the imposition of conditions and structures that hamper development. Periodically, debts may need rescheduling or even remission; this must be done judiciously, so that future credit is not inhibited. Traditional land rights should be respected as far as compatible with economic realities; as fewer people work on the land and mobility increases, our ultimate dependence on its resources and our love for it must find fresh ways of expression. No system is perfect, and inevitably some will enrich themselves at the expense of others; some will be placed under the domination of others; from time to time we must be ready to make the necessary adjustments to bring freedom to all, in joy, peace, and common humanity.

The contribution offered by Judaism, in the company of other religious traditions, is to call for the implementation of justice and compassion within the present order, to stimulate the "technicians" to devise means for the creation and distribution of wealth that are morally superior and more efficient than those we now have, and to act as a constant witness to the universal values that attest God's presence in His world.

Classical Sources of Judaism

Bible (Hebrew Scriptures). The best recent Jewish translation is that of the Jewish Publication Society (2nd ed.; Philadelphia, 1999). It is a collaborative venture of scholars and rabbis from the main branches of Judaism, and parts of it appeared as early as 1962.

Mishna. This has the form of a law code and was compiled around 215 C.E. in Palestine. It is elaborated further in the Tosefta and in the two Talmudim (plural of Talmud), that of the Land of Israel, completed around 450 C.E., and the more influential Babylonian Talmud, completed around 550 C.E.

The term Midrash, or "interpretation," is used for various works of biblical interpretation, both *halakhic* ("to do with law") and *aggadic* ("homiletic").

English translations of most of these works are widely available.

After the "classical" period the development of the law was expressed in responsa (replies to questions addressed to rabbis and religious judges), and from time to time full codifications were compiled, the best know being those of Maimonides and Karo referred to in the essay.

Discussion Questions

1. Some nations have a per capita income more than a hundred times higher than other nations. To what extent does the responsibility for adjusting this inequity devolve upon (a) individuals, (b) governments, (c) multinational corporations, (d) religious bodies?

2. Is it feasible or desirable to abolish the payment of interest on money loans? Are the Jewish system of *heter 'iska* and the Islamic *Qirad* genuine alternatives to "the system" or merely legal fictions to disguise interest payments?

3. Leviticus 19:18 says, "Love your neighbor as yourself." This is great ethical teaching, but how does it help solve the practical issues of the fair distribution of wealth?

4. The Hebrew Scriptures constantly stress the relationship of people and land. What are the consequences for this relationship when we consider growing populations and changing patterns of land utilization?

5. Can we conclude from the biblical laws of the Jubilee (Leviticus 25) that we ought periodically to cancel all Third-World debts?

SUGGESTED FURTHER READINGS

Large tracts of the Bible, especially the writings of the prophets, are devoted to social justice. Samples: Leviticus 25; Deuteronomy 16:18-20; 1 Kings 21; Psalm 1; Psalm 94; Isaiah 5:8; Isaiah 32; Amos 2. For an understanding of the prophetic concept of justice, see chapter 11 of A. J. Heschel's The Prophets, *listed below.*

Heschel, Abraham Joshua, *The Prophets*. New York: Harper & Row, 1962. Chapter 11 is an excellent introduction to the prophetic concept of justice.

Siegel, Seymour, "A Jewish View of Economic Justice." In *Contemporary Jewish Ethics and Morality: A Reader*, ed. Elliot N. Dorff and Louis E. Newman. New York: Oxford University Press, 1995, pp. 336-443.

Solomon, Norman, *Judaism and World Religion*. New York: St. Martin's Press, 1991. Chapters 2-4.

Chapter 6

God's Household: Christianity, Economics, and Planetary Living

By Sallie McFague

Abstract

Religions help us form the basic assumptions about who we are and how we should act in the world. Presently, two worldviews with accompanying economic rules for planetary living vie for our loyalty. One is the neoclassical market model with its ideology of greed and its goal of growth: the consumer society. The other is the ecological economic model with its creed of interdependence and its goal of planetary sustainability: the just society. Many Christians, particularly middle-class North Americans, are presently captive to the first model. Christianity should, however, advocate the second model—the one that sees the good of all beings, including human beings, as dependent on a sustainable planet where resources are justly distributed. The ecological economic model is not Christian economics; rather, it is an economic model that faintly resembles the radical inclusiveness and open table of Jesus' Kingdom of God. It is better than the market model for human beings and the planet. It is also a more appropriate one for Christians to support.

Religion and Economics

None of the world's major religions has as its maxim: "Blessed are the greedy." Given the many differences among religions on doctrines and practice, it is remarkable to find widespread agreement at the level of economics. Often, however, religion is not considered to be *about* economics; in fact, many in most societies do not want religion to intrude into economics. It is preferable, they say, for religion to attend to "religious matters" and leave economics to the economists.

But most religions know better. They know that economics is about human well-being, about who eats and who does not, who has clothes and shelter and who does not, who has the basics for a decent life and who does not. Economics is about life and death, as well as the quality of life. Economics is not just about money, but about sharing scarce resources among all who need them.

Economics is a justice issue, so why would religions not be concerned with it?

In many religions the concern for justice has been focused on human beings—and this is certainly the case in Christianity, at least for the last few centuries. But recently, the issues of well-being and justice have been extended to embrace the entire planet. The well-being of the planet and of its people is increasingly seen to be inextricably related. In Christianity, there is a return to the cosmological context for interpreting the faith rather than the narrow psychological focus prevalent since the Reformation. In fact, many current Christian theologies embrace all three of the classical interpretive contexts: the cosmological, the political, and the personal (Hendry 1980, chapter 1). That is, Christian faith embraces the *world*—all of creation and not just human beings who make up less than one percent of it. The Redeemer is also the Creator: all of creation, including dying nature as well as oppressed people, are within God's "economy," God's "household."

It is no coincidence that the Greek word for house, *oikos*, is the source of our words for economics, ecology, and ecumenical. The three belong together: in order for the whole household of the planet to flourish, the earth's resources must be distributed justly among all its inhabitants, human and earth others, on a sustainable basis. The three basic economic rules for all to thrive in this household are: take only your share; clean up after yourself; and keep the house in good repair for those to come. These rules should be pinned up on the planet's "fridge" for all members to memorize and follow. They are necessities, not suggestions, that constitute the basic economic laws for long-term planetary well-being.

But this economic paradigm is certainly not the dominant one in global society today. Nor is it the one that most Christians seem to be embracing. To be sure, Christians do not openly support "Blessed are the greedy." Nonetheless, that is the way most of us live. Why? Quite simply, because we are members of a society, now a worldwide one, that accepts, almost without question, an economic theory that supports insatiable greed on the part of individuals. This theory lies behind present-day market capitalism and, since the death of communism and the decline of socialism, it is accepted by most ordinary people as a description of the way things are and must be. Market capitalism is seen as the "truth." Although it is a "description of the way things are" in our society, it is not a description of the way things must be—or should be. Market capitalism is a type of economics that allocates scarce resources on the basis of individuals successfully competing for them, not with regard to the needs of the planet's inhabitants nor with an eye to its sustainability. It is an economic model which makes a case for how scarce resources might be allocated, not a description of how they must be allocated.

This realization—that economics is not a "hard" science, but an ideology with an assumed anthropology and goal for the planet (summarized by greed and growth)—is the first step in seeing things otherwise. Ecological economics—economics for the well-being of the whole household of planet Earth and all its creatures—is also a model with an anthropological and planetary ideology. This model claims that human beings, while greedy to be sure, are even more needy. After all, they, we, depend on the health of all the other parts of the planet for our very existence: clean water, breathable air, arable land, plants, etc. Ecological economics claims that market capitalism denies one huge fact: unless the limited resources of the planet are justly distributed among its myriad life forms so they all can flourish, there will be no sustainable future for even the greediest among us. We cannot live without these other sources of our existence; we can live only a few minutes without air, a few days without water, a few weeks without food. Of all creatures alive, we are the neediest.

CHRISTIANITY AND ECONOMICS

Is ecological economics "Christian" economics? No, not in any one-on-one or exclusive sense. It is, however, an emerging economic model that is being increasingly set forth and supported by a wide range of NGOs (nongovernmental organizations) and protest movements. As reported recently in the press, the motto of ecological economics is "a different world is possible," and its basic tenets are concern for fair labor laws and environmental health. Lynn White's oft-quoted essay lays the blame for environmental deterioration at the feet of religion, specifically Christianity (White 1967, 1203-7). If Christianity was capable of doing such immense damage, then surely the restoration of nature must also lie, at least in part, with Christianity. I believe it does, but also with other world religions as well as with education, government, economics, and science. The environmental crisis creates a "planetary agenda," involving all people, all areas of expertise, all religions.

This is the case because the environmental crisis is not a "problem" that any specialization can solve. Rather it is about how we—all of us human beings and all other creatures—can live justly and sustainably on our planet. It is about the "house rules" that will enable us to do so. These rules include attitudes as well as technologies, behaviors as well as science. They are what the *oikos*, the house we all share, demands that we think and do so there will be enough for everyone. The "house rules" are concerned with the management of the resources of planet Earth so that all may thrive indefinitely.

How does religion and specifically Christianity fit into this picture? It fits where all religions do: at the point of the worldview underlying the house rules. It fits at the level of the deeply held and often largely unconscious assumptions about who we are in the scheme of things and how we should act.[1] While anthropology is not the only concern of religions, it is a central one and, for the purposes of the ecological crisis, the one that may count the most.

This chapter will attempt to make the case that Christianity, at least since the Protestant Reformation and especially since the Enlightenment, has through its individualistic view of human life,

[1] Marcus J. Borg describes this well: "A root image is a fundamental 'picture' of reality. Perhaps most often called a 'world-view,' it consists of our most taken-for-granted assumptions about what is possible. . . . Very importantly, a root image not only provides a model of reality, but also shapes our perception and our thinking, operating almost unconsciously within us as a dim background affecting all of our seeing and thinking. A root image thus functions as both an image and a lens: it is a picture of reality which becomes a lens through which we see reality." Borg 1994, 127.

implicitly and sometimes explicitly, supported the neoclassical economic paradigm. This paradigm has led to the current consumer culture, which is devastating the planet and widening the gap between the rich and the poor.[2] As an alternative, we will suggest that Christianity, given its oldest and deepest anthropology, should support an ecological economic model, one in which our well-being is seen as interrelated and interdependent with the well-being of all other living things and earth processes.[3] At the moment, Christianity is not advocating such a model. Indeed, it is the claim of this chapter that the individualistic anthropology that is deep within our consumer-oriented culture is supported not only by government and contemporary economics but also by religion.[4] When these three major institutions present a united front, a sacred canopy is cast over a society, validating the behavior of its people. It is difficult to believe that science and technology alone can solve an ecological crisis supported by this triumvirate which legitimizes human beings continuing to feel, think, and act in ways that are contrary to the just distribution of the world's resources and the sustainability of the planet.

[2] The literature on the neoclassical economic model and its alternative—what I am calling the ecological economic model—is large and growing. Some of the works I found most helpful are as follows: Brown et al.; Costanza et al. 1997; Crocker and Linden 1998; Daly and Cobb 1994; Daly 1996; Goodwin, Ackerman, and Kirion 1997; Hackett 1998; Rasmussen 1996; Rieger 1998; *United Nations Human Development Report* (New York: Oxford University Press), issued annually; Zweig 1991.

[3] By the oldest and deepest anthropology, I am referring to what George Hendry calls the "cosmological" and "political" understandings of God and the world rather than the more recent and narrow "psychological" view. The latter, which supports individualism, has arisen in the last several hundred years, but the other two, one emphasizing the whole creation and the other the community of all human beings, are grounded in the Hebrew Scriptures as well as in the New Testament and early theology (especially Irenaeus and Augustine). See Hendry 1980.

[4] The evidence supporting this claim would take considerable space to lay out. Suffice it to say here that both the born-again and New Age versions of popular religion do so; the American Declaration of Independence's "life, liberty, and the pursuit of happiness" does; and Adam Smith's description of the human being as a creature of insatiable greed makes a significant contribution. All focus on the rights, desires, and needs of individuals.

Neoclassical and Ecological Economics

The two worldviews—neoclassical economic(s) and ecological economic(s)—are dramatically different; consequently, they have different anthropologies and different house rules. The first model sees human beings on the planet as a corporation or syndicate, a collection of individuals drawn together to benefit its members by optimal use of natural resources. The second model sees the planet more like an organism or a community that survives and prospers through the interdependence of all its parts, human and non-human. The first model rests on assumptions from the eighteenth-century view of human beings as individuals with rights and responsibilities and of the world as a machine or collection of individual parts, related externally to one another. The second model rests on assumptions from postmodern science in its view of human beings as the conscious and radically dependent part of the planet and of the world as a community or organism, internally related in all its parts. Both are models, interpretations of the world and our place in it: neither is a description of fact. This point must be underscored because the first model seems natural, indeed inevitable and true to most middle-class Westerners, while the second model seems novel, perhaps even utopian or fanciful. In fact, both come from assumptions of different historical periods; both are world-pictures built on these assumptions, and each vies for our agreement and loyalty.

We will suggest that the syndicate or machine model is injurious to nature and to poor people, while the other one, the community or organic model, is healthier for the planet and all its inhabitants. In other words, we need to assess the "economy" of both models, their notions of the allocation of scare resources to family members, to determine which view of the "good life" is better.

The mention of allocation of scarce resources brings us to the heart of the matter. The reason economics is so important, why it is a religious and ecological issue, is that it is not just a matter of money; rather, it is a matter of survival and flourishing. Economics is a value issue. In making economic decisions, the "bottom line" is not the only consideration. Many other values are present in decisions concerning scarce resources: from the health of a community to its recreational opportunities; from the beauty of other life forms to our concern for their well-being; from a desire to see our children fed and clothed to a sense of responsibility for the welfare of future generations.

Contemporary neoclassical economists, however, generally deny that economics is about values.[5] But this denial is questionable. By neoclassical economics we mean market capitalism as conceived by Adam Smith in the eighteenth century and, more particularly, the version of it practiced by the major economies of our time. The key feature of market capitalism is the allocation of scarce resources by means of decentralized markets: allocation occurs as the result of individual market transactions each of which is guided by self-interest (Hackett 1998, 33). At the base of neoclassical economics is an anthropology: human beings are individuals motivated by self-interest. The value by which scarce resources are allocated, then, is the fulfillment of the self-interest of human beings. The assumption is that each person will act to maximize her or his own interest, and by doing so all will eventually benefit from the so-called invisible hand of classical economic theory.

Neoclassical economics has one value: the monetary fulfillment of individuals provided they compete successfully for the resources. But what of other values? Two key ones, if we have the economics of the entire planet in mind, are the just distribution of the earth's resources and the ability of the planet to sustain our use of its resources. However, these matters—distributive justice to the world's inhabitants and the optimal scale of the human economy within the planet's economy—are considered "external-

[5] Milton Friedman's distinction between "positive" and "normative" economics is typical: "Normative economics is speculative and personal, a matter of values and preferences that are beyond science. Economics as a science, as a tool for understanding and prediction, must be based solely on positive economics which 'is in principle independent of any particular ethical position or normative judgments.'" See Friedman 1953, 4.

ities" by neoclassical economics (Daly 1996, 50ff.). In other words, the issues of who benefits from an economic system and whether the planet can bear the system's burden are not part of neoclassical economics.

In sum, the worldview or basic assumption of neoclassical economics is surprisingly simple and straightforward: human beings are self-interested individuals who, acting on this basis, will create a syndicate or corporation, even a global one, capable of benefiting all eventually. Hence, as long as the economy grows, individuals in a society will sooner or later participate in prosperity. These assumptions about human nature are scarcely value-neutral. They indicate a preference for a certain view of who we are and what the goal of human effort should be: the view of human nature is individualism and the goal is economic growth.

When we turn to the alternative ecological economic paradigm we see a different set of values. Are we basically greedy or needy? Probably both, but as our answers veer toward one pole or the other, we will find ourselves embracing an individualistic or a community model of life. Ecological economics claims we cannot survive (even to be greedy) unless we acknowledge our profound dependence on one another and the earth. Human need is more basic than human greed: we are relational beings from the moment of our conception to our last breath. The well-being of the individual is inextricably connected to the well-being of the whole.

These two interpretations of who we are and where we fit in the world are almost mirror opposites of each other on the three critical issues of allocation of resources, distributive justice, and sustainability. Neoclassical economics begins with the unconstrained allocation of resources to competing individuals, on the assumption that if all people operate from this base, issues of fair distribution and sustainability will eventually work themselves out. Ecological economics begins with the viability of the whole community, on the assumption that only as it thrives now and in the future will its various members, including human beings, thrive as well. In other words, ecological economics begins with sustainability and distributive justice, not with the allocation of resources among competing individuals. Before all else the community must be able to survive (sustainability), which it can do only if all members have the use of resources (distributive justice). Then, within these parameters, the allocation of scarce resources among competing users can take place.

Ecological economics does not pretend to be value-free; its preference is evident: the well-being and sustainability of our household, planet Earth. It recognizes the *oikos* base of ecology, economics, and ecumenicity: economics is the management of a community's physical necessities for the benefit of all. Ecological economics is a human enterprise that seeks to maximize the optimal functioning of the planet's gifts and services for all users. Ecological economics, then, is first of all a vision of how human beings ought to live on planet Earth in light of the perceived reality of where and how we live. We live in, with, and from the earth. This story of who we are is based on postmodern science, not as in neoclassical economics, on the eighteenth-century story of reality.

Neoclassical or Ecological Economics: Which Is Good for Planet Earth?

In addressing this question, we are concerning ourselves with the most important of the three economic issues: sustainability. Can neoclassical economics as currently understood sustain the planet? In the neoclassical economic view the world is a machine or syndicate; presumably then, when some parts give out they can be replaced with substitutes. If, for instance, our main ecological problem is nonrenewable resources (oil, coal, minerals, etc.), then human ingenuity might well fill in the gaps when they occur. Since the earth is considered an externality by many neoclassical economics, then "good for the planet" can only mean good for human beings to use. Sustainability is not the major priority.

The state of our planet at the beginning of the new millennium, however, is far different than simply the loss of nonrenewable resources. In fact, that problem is of less importance than two other related ones: the rate of loss of renewable resources and the manner in which these losses overlap and support further deterioration. The big problems are the loss of water, trees, fertile soil, clean air, fisheries, and biodiversity, *and* the ways the degradation of each of these renewables contributes to the deterioration of the rest. In other words, if the planet is seen more like an organism than a machine, with all parts interrelated and interdependent, then after a certain level of decay of its various members, it will, like any body, become sick at its core, sick to the point of not functioning properly. It will not be able to sustain itself.

This is widely known as the "synergism of planetary operation." The various parts of the planet as an organism work together both in health and in decay to create something both better and worse than the individual parts. When the various members of an ecosystem are healthy, they work together to provide innumerable free services that none could do alone and that we take for granted: materials production (food, fisheries, timber, genetic resources, medicines), pollination, biological control of pests and diseases, habitat and refuge, water supply and regulation, waste recycling and pollution control, educational/scientific resources, recreation (Abramowitz 1997). These services are essential to our survival and well-being; they can continue only if we sustain them. This list of services should be seen as a web: none of them can function alone—each depends on the others. These services are part of the "commons" of our world community. They constitute our very lifeblood that we hold in trust for future generations.

The most important services are not necessarily the most visible ones. For instance, in a forest it is not only the standing trees that are valuable but also the fallen ones (the nurse logs on which new trees grow); the habitat the forest provides for birds and insects that pollinate crops and destroy diseases; the plants that provide biodiversity for food and medicines; the forest canopy that breaks the force of winds; the roots that reduce soil erosion; the photosynthesis of plants that helps stabilize the climate. The smallest providers—the insects, worms, spiders, fungi, algae, and bacteria—are critically important in creating a stable, sustainable home for humans and other creatures. If such a forest is clear-cut to harvest the trees, everything else goes as well. All these services disappear. A healthy ecosystem—complex and diverse in all its features, both large and small—is resilient like a well-functioning body. A simplified, degraded nature, supporting single-species crops in ruined soil with inadequate water and violent weather events, results in a diminished environment for human beings as well. "The bottom line is that for humans to be healthy and resilient, nature must be too" (Abramowitz 1997, 109).

An economic model that does not have as its first priority the sustainability of the planet cannot be good for human beings. The neoclassical market model does not have such a priority. Hence, it is not good for us *even if we like it*. We are addicted to our consumer lifestyle, and we are in denial that it is bad for us and for our planet. But of even greater importance, it is *unjust*: many of the world's people have been impoverished by this model. As things now stand, some of us are consuming *much* more, while others are consuming less. According to the United Nations *Human Development Report* (1998), 20 percent of people in high-income countries account for 86 percent of private consumption while the poorest 20 percent of the world's population consume only 1.3 percent of the pie. In Africa, the average household consumes 20 percent less than it did 25 years ago. Furthermore, two-thirds of the world's population lives on less than two dollars per day.

CHRISTIANITY AND THE ECOLOGICAL ECONOMIC MODEL

The model we need is very different. To recall, the ecological model claims that housemates must abide by three main rules: take only your share, clean up after yourselves, and keep the house in good repair for future occupants. We don't own this house; we don't even rent it. It is loaned to us for our lifetime with the proviso that we must obey the rules so that it can continue to feed, shelter, nurture, and delight others. These rules are not laws that we can circumvent or disobey; they are the conditions of our existence, and they are intrinsic to our happiness.

If we were to follow these rules we would be living within a different vision of the good life, the abundant life, than is current in our consumer culture and that is destroying the planet. We would begin to accept what ecological economist Robert Costanza calls our greatest calling: "Probably the most challenging task facing humanity today is the creation of a shared vision of a sustainable and desirable society, one that can provide permanent prosperity within the biophysical constraints of the real world in a way that is fair and equitable to all of humanity, to other species, and to future generations" (Costanza et al. 1997, 179).

Which of the two worldviews expresses the values inherent in Christianity? Does it matter? Yes, it does if one accepts the assumption of this paper that worldviews matter. While there is no direct connection between believing and acting, thinking and doing, there is an implicit, deeper, and more insidious one: the worldview that persuades us that it is natural and inevitable becomes the secret partner of our decisions and actions.

Moreover, a persuasive case can be made that there is an intrinsic connection between the ecological economic model and Christianity. Distributive justice and sustainability, as goals for planetary living, are pale reflections, but reflections nonetheless, of what Jesus meant by the Kingdom of God (Borg 1994). Let us look at the vivid portrait of Jesus by New Testament scholar John Dominic Crossan: "The open commensality and radical egalitarianism of Jesus' Kingdom of God are more terrifying than anything we have ever imagined, and even if we can never accept it, we should not explain it away as something else" (Crossan 1994, 73-74). For Jesus, the Kingdom of God was epitomized by everyone being invited to the table; the Kingdom is known by radical equality at the level of bodily needs. Crossan names the Parable of the Feast as central to understanding what Jesus means by the Kingdom of God. This is a shocking story, trespassing society's boundaries of class, gender, status, and ethnicity—as its end result is inviting *all* to the feast. There are several versions (Matt. 22:1-13; Luke 14:15-24; Gospel of Thomas 64), but in each a prominent person invites other, presumably worthy, people to a banquet, only to have them refuse: one to survey a land purchase, another to try out some new oxen, a third to attend a wedding. The frustrated host then tells his servants to go out into the streets of the city and bring whomever they find to dinner: the poor, maimed, blind, lame, good, and bad (the list varies in the three versions). The shocking implication is that everyone—*anyone*—is invited. As Crossan remarks, if beggars come to your door, you might give them food or even invite them into the kitchen for a meal, but you don't ask them to join the family in the dining room or invite them back on Saturday night for supper with your friends. But that is exactly what happens in this story. The Kingdom of God, according to Crossan's portrait of Jesus, is "more terrifying than anything we have imagined" (Crossan 1994, 68) because it demolishes all our carefully constructed boundaries between the worthy and the unworthy and does so at the most physical, bodily level.

For first-century Jews, the key boundary was purity laws: one did not eat with the poor, women, the diseased, or the unrighteous. For us, the critical barrier is economic: one is not called to sustainable and just sharing of resources with the poor, the disadvantaged, the lazy. To do otherwise, in both cultures, is improper, not expected—in fact, shocking. And yet, in both cases, the issue is the most basic bodily one—who is invited to share the food? In other words: who lives and who dies? In both cases, the answer is the same: everyone, regardless of status (by any criteria), is invited. This vision of God's will for the world does not specifically mention just, sustainable planetary living, but throughout the Bible, Holy Scripture surely is more in line with that worldview than it is with the satisfaction of individual consumer desires.

Unlike our first-century Mediterranean counterparts, North American middle-class Christians are not terrified by the unclean, but we are by the poor. There are so many of them—billions! Surely we cannot be expected to share the planet's resources justly and sustainably with all of them. Yet, this historical Jesus appears to disagree: he is not, it seems, interested so much in religion, including his own, as in human well-being, beginning with the body: feeding the hungry and healing the suffering. Moreover, his message, according to Crossan, had less to do with what Jesus did for others than what others might do for their neighbors: "The Kingdom of God was not, for Jesus, a divine monopoly exclusively bound to his own person. It began at the level of the body and appeared as a shared community of healing and eating—that is to say, of spiritual and physical resources available to each and all without distinctions, discrimination, or hierarchies. One entered the Kingdom as a way of life and anyone who could live it could bring it to others. It was not just words alone, or deeds alone, but both together as life-style" (Crossan 1994, 113-14).

The body is the locus: how we treat needy bodies gives the clue to how a society is organized. It suggests that correct "table manners" are a sign of a just society, the Kingdom of God. If one accepts this interpretation, the table becomes not primarily the priestly consecrated bread and wine of communion celebrating Jesus' death for the sins of the world, but rather the egalitarian meals of bread and fishes that one finds throughout Jesus' ministry (Crossan 1994, 79-81). At these events, all are invited to share in the food, whether it be meager or sumptuous. Were this understanding of the Eucharist to infiltrate Christian churches today, it could be mind-changing—in fact, maybe world-changing.

At the very least, such an understanding would be terrifying. Would it also be absurd, foolish, and utopian? Perhaps, but, as we have suggested, there appears to be a degree of continuity between this reconstruction of society—the Kingdom of God—and what we have described as the ecological economic worldview. This worldview is closer to that terrifying picture of sharing our food with the poor than is the neoclassical economic model. We might see this continuity as the ideal and the pale reflection of God's Kingdom; perhaps just, sustainable planetary living is a foretaste, a glimmer, an inkling of the Kingdom of God.

If this is the case, then for middle-class, North American Christians in so-called developed nations, it may well be that a primary form of sin is refusing to acknowledge the link between the Kingdom and the ecological economic worldview, explaining the obvious connection away because of the consequences for our privileged lifestyle. And yet we cannot ignore that sustainability and the just distribution of resources are concerned with human and planetary well-being for all. This is, we suggest, the responsible interpretation of the Parable of the Feast for affluent North American Christians living in the twenty-first century. It demands that we look at the systemic structures separating the haves and the have-nots in our time. They are the collective forms of our sin.

They are the institutions, laws, and international bodies of market capitalism (often aided by the silence of the churches) that allow some to get richer and most to become poorer. Our sin is one of commission but perhaps more damningly of omission: our greed camouflaged by indifference and denial—and even by our good works of charity for the "uninvited."

Next Steps: A Christian Response to the Environmental Crisis

In order to dislodge the neoclassical economic worldview and Christianity's complicity with it, four steps are needed:

The first step is becoming conscious that neoclassical economics is a model, not a description, of how to allocate scarce resources. There are other ways to live, other ways to divide things up, other goals for human beings and the planet. "Economics" is always necessary, but not necessarily neoclassical economics: ecological economics is an alternative.

The second step is to suggest some visions of the good life that are not consumer dominated, visions that are just and sustainable. Such visions could include the basic necessities for all, universal medical care and education, opportunities for creativity and meaningful work, time for family and friends, green spaces in cities, and wilderness for other creatures. We need to ask what really makes people happy and which of these visions are just to the world's inhabitants and sustainable for the planet.

A third step is for well-off Christians to publicly advocate the ecological model as the more just and sustainable one for our planet. Specifically, this means becoming informed about the global injustices of market economies; joining with other NGOs to change the policies and practices of so-called free trade that result in impoverishment and unsustainability; and accepting the consequence for our own lifestyle that sharing earth's resources more justly and sustainably will entail. While no human economic system can be the Kingdom of God, Christians have the obligation to work for systems that are at least faint approximations, rather than in clear opposition, to it.

The fourth step is to rethink what the ecological economic

context would mean for the basic doctrines of Christianity: God and the world, Christ and salvation, human life and discipleship.

While this last task is beyond the scope of this paper, let us end with a few brief comments about God and the world, because this is at the heart of who we think we are and what we should do. Since our interpretive context, the ecological economic model, is about the just and sustainable allocation of resources among all planetary users, the framework for speaking of God and the world becomes worldly well-being. Or, to phrase it in terms of a gloss on Irenaeus: "The glory of God is every creature fully alive." Dietrich Bonhoeffer called it "worldly Christianity." He said that God is neither a metaphysical abstraction nor the answer to gaps in our knowledge—God is neither in the sky nor on the fringes but at "the center of the village," in the midst of life, both its pains and its joys (Bonhoeffer 1960, letter of April 30, 1944). An ecological economic model means an earthly God, an incarnate God, a truly immanent God.

As we look, then, at the big picture, the general outline of this theology, we find it basically different from the theology implied by the neoclassical model. Broadly speaking, the differences can be suggested as a movement toward the earth: from heaven to earth; from the otherworldly to this worldly; from above to below; from a distant, external God to a near, truly immanent God; from time and history to space and land; from soul to body; from individualism to community; from mechanistic to organic thinking; from spiritual salvation to holistic well-being; from anthropocentrism to cosmocentrism. The ecological model means a shift not from God to the world, but from a distant God related externally to the world to an embodied God who is the source of the world's life and fulfillment.

The neoclassical economic model assumes God, like the human being, is an individual; in fact, the super-individual who controls the world through laws of nature, much as a good mechanic makes a well-designed machine operate efficiently. This God is at the beginning (creation) and intervenes from time to time to influence personal and public history, but is otherwise absent from the world. The ecological model, on the contrary, claims that God is radically present in the world, as close as the breath, the joy, and the suffering of every creature. The two views of God and the world, then, are very different: in the one, God's power is evident in God's distant control of the world; in the other, God's glory is manifest in God's total self-giving to the world.

In closing, let us note that two pictures of God and the world suggest different answers to the question Who are we and what should we do? In the first, we are individuals responsible to a transcendent God who rewards or punishes according to our merits and God's mercy. In the second, we are beings-in-community living in the presence of God who is the power and love in everything that exists. In the first, we should do what is fair to other individuals while taking care of our own well-being; in the second, we should do what is necessary to work with God to create a just and sustainable planet, for only in that way will all flourish. This is the great work of the twenty-first century. Never before have we had to think of everyone and everything all together. We now know that if we are to survive and our planet flourish, we will do so as a whole or not at all. Christians believe we do not have to do this alone: "I came to you that you might have life and have it abundantly" (John 10:10).

DISCUSSION QUESTIONS

1. What is the difference between economics as a "hard science" and economics as an "ideology"?

2. Describe and discuss the difference between "neoclassical economics" and "ecological economics."

3. Discuss the significance and feasibility of the "three house rules" for a sustainable economics and the flourishing of life on earth.

4. ". . . it may well be that a primary form of sin is refusing to acknowledge the link between [Jesus' view of] the Kingdom and the ecological economic worldview. . . ." Discuss the meaning of this statement and whether you agree.

5. Describe and discuss the different understandings of God that support the ecological and the neoclassical economic models.

Suggested Further Reading

Costanza, Robert, et al. *An Introduction to Ecological Economics.* Boca Raton, Fla.: St. Lucie Press, 1997.

Daly, Herman E. *Beyond Growth: The Economics of Sustainable Development.* Boston: Beacon Press, 1996.

McFague, Sallie. *Life Abundant: Rethinking Theology and Economics for a Planet in Peril.* Minneapolis: Fortress Press, 2001.

Chapter 7

Globalization and Greed: A Muslim Perspective

By Ameer Ali

Abstract

The concept of globalization has gained hegemonic currency in theoretical and political discourse. The first part of this paper analyzes the economic dimension of this concept, traces its links with the philosophy of economic liberalism, and assesses its achievements and failures. In the second part, the challenge of Islam to global capitalism and the ruling economic order is viewed in the light of Islamic beliefs and Muslim history. Ideal Islam is compared with Islam in practice, and the difficulties that Islam is facing to achieve its ideal objectives are briefly explained. The paper concludes with a sense of optimism that the Islamic objectives have much in common with those of other religions and a universal collective effort is a possibility to overcome the shortcomings of global capitalism.

What Is Globalization?

Globalization, a word first introduced in 1961 and since the 1980s translated into several other languages, has now become a communicative catchword dominating the current dialogue among intellectuals, economists, politicians, and journalists. In general the word now describes a socioeconomic paradigm just like "postmodernism" in the 1970s and "modernization" after the second world war. The understanding of what globalization is remains fluid. In his critical introduction to globalization, Jan Aart Scholte identifies four of the most popular definitions and found all of them redundant because of their overlapping substance. As he argues, to define globalization as internalization, liberalization, universalization, and westernization or modernization adds nothing unique in substance to warrant a new terminology. He therefore introduces a fifth term, "supraterritoriality" or "deterritorialization," in order to underline the most salient characteristic of globalization, the erosion of national characteristics of human activity (Scholte 2000, 15-16). Sociologists like Malcolm

Waters define globalization as "a social process in which the constraints of geography on social and cultural arrangements recede and in which people become increasingly aware that they are receding" (Waters 1996, 3). In other words, the process of globalization, as Zygmunt Bauman explains, has devalued time and space in the material sense (Bauman 1998, 6-17; Bauman 2000, 91-129). Globalization in this respect has come to mean *a borderless world.*

In its economic sense, however, globalization signifies the domination of the capitalist economic dogma on a scale unprecedented in modern history. Capitalism, as an economic system, has proved to the world its remarkable power of resilience and adaptation to changing political, economic, and technological environments. Although it remains intransigent in its fundamental assumptions about human motives and in its belief in the efficiency of free markets, the institutional framework within which that system operates has continued to change in the face of both internal and external challenges. Thus, the competitive capitalism of the eighteenth and nineteenth centuries, as theorized by the classical economists in an environment of mostly homogenous but small-scale production and exchange units, was transformed into monopoly capitalism in the twentieth century. In their pioneering research into monopoly capitalism, Paul Baran and Paul M. Sweezy identified the rise of oligopolies and economies of large-scale production as its crucial determinants (Baran and Sweezy 1968). Since the closing decades of the twentieth century, the world is witnessing yet another transformation, but this time to a more radical and dynamic phase, described by Edward Luttwak as "turbo capitalism" (Luttwak 1999). In this latest phase, many economies and most of their economic activities are freeing themselves from their national and nationalistic constraints and are increasingly assuming a deterritorial or supranational magnitude, although without a global authority to govern them. Without a "global state" and a "global government," global capitalism is becoming increasingly "disorganized" (Beck 2000, 11-13). It is the global scale of this transformation that adds the economic dimension to the phenomenon of globalization. Some analysts even see in this the birth of a "New Leviathan" (Ross and Trachte 1990). In short, economic globalization and the global economy are often perceived as synonymous with global capitalism.

Economic Liberalism

The essence of economic globalization or global capitalism is its philosophy of liberalism, which advocates "individual freedom to own and inherit property, to choose one's own occupation, and to profit from one's own abilities" (Self 2000, 35). It is a philosophy based on self-interest, and it was Adam Smith, the Scottish moral philosopher and the father of classical economics, who first developed the economic theory of liberalism in his historic work *An Inquiry into the Nature and Causes of the Wealth of Nations*, published in 1776. (Coincidentally, 1776 was also the year of the American Declaration of Independence, and it is the United States that is now in the forefront of championing the cause of globalization.)

"It is not from the benevolence of the butcher, the brewer, or the baker that we expect our dinner," Smith wrote, "but from their regard to their own interest. We address ourselves, not to their humanity but to their self-love, and never talk to them of our own necessities but of their advantages" (Smith 1981, book I, 12).

It is in the relentless pursuit of one's self-interest that economic liberalism finds a panacea for human progress and economic prosperity. If every individual in a society, whether as a consumer, producer, or an exchanger, is allowed, without outside interference, to take care of his or her self-interest, the cumulative effect of their individual endeavors, according to Smith's philosophy, will be the greatest happiness of the greatest number. "The pursuit of individual advantage," said David Ricardo, the originator of the principle of comparative advantage, "is admirably connected with the universal good of the whole" (Ricardo 1993, 81). In modern theoretical parlance "atomistic individualism" leads to economic efficiency and societal progress.

The mechanism that promotes the achievement of this efficiency and progress is Adam Smith's concept of the "invisible hand," or the natural market forces. Any interference in the operation of the market, according to the philosophy of liberalism, will hinder progress and create inefficiency. Only when the market fails, as in the case of providing "pure" public goods such as national defense, can there be any justification for interference. It is because of their general antagonism against government interference in economic matters that would otherwise be provided more efficiently by the private sector that the advocates of economic globalization are also known as the free marketeers.

Objectively speaking, who or what can interfere in the operation of the market? In general, there are two groups or forces that can act as constraints. First, a society's historical traditions, ethical and moral values, and religious beliefs can, at times, control and guide individual enterprise in the interest of a larger group or higher ideals. However, if these traditions, values, and beliefs are irrational and not scientifically objective, then they are an obstacle rather than a stimulus to achieve efficiency. This is why economic thinkers of the neoclassical variety dismiss ethical and moral considerations in economic analysis and prefer to call their discipline a "positive science." It was Nassau Senior, another classical economist, who first argued the case for a value-free science of economics. The neoclassicals zealously continued this tradition, and now under economic rationalism, "The economist's task," as J. K. Galbraith observes with a great sense of cynicism, "is to stand apart, analyze, describe and where possible reduce to mathematical formulae, but not to pass moral judgement or be otherwise involved" (Galbraith 1987, 124). Globalization embraces this stance and wants the market to be free of all cultural and ethical encumbrances.

The second source of constraint arises from government actions. Over the last two hundred years or more, governments have intervened in the operation of the market in two distinct ways. On the one hand, they have legislated to regulate the market so that unfair producer competition and consumer exploitation could be minimized if not totally eliminated. On the other hand, they have intervened and provided budgetary resources to enhance market competition and economic efficiency. A free market that operates competitively is expected to maximize economic output by minimizing resource cost. Economists of both the classical and neoclassical variety argue that the conflict between the profit-maximizing behavior of the producer and the utility-maximizing behavior of the consumer will drive the economy toward efficiency and promote economic growth. This is the strongest case for economic liberalism, and any rule or regulation that a government designs to promote this behavior is welcomed by the free-market ideologues.

However, a competitive market is at its weakest when it comes to issues about economic distribution and social justice. This negative side of economic liberalism explains why governments were forced to intervene in a third way and implement measures to remedy the injustices of the market. The evolution of the welfare state in the twentieth century, which is now under assault by the same ideologues, is the result of this type of intervention.[1] Globalization and its underlying philosophy of liberalism condemn the first and third types of intervention. Hence, the cry from the free marketeers for the privatization of state enterprises; removal of state control over trade, banking and finance; microeconomic reforms in the commodity and factor markets; reduction in welfare expenditure; and, ultimately, a gradual recoiling of the state as an economic agent.

Achievements and Failures of Globalization

What are the achievements of globalization? First, by successfully removing a large number of quantitative barriers to trade, globalization has enabled the residents in one country to consume a large variety of products made in another country. Second, by relaxing state control over finance and banking, globalization has made it possible for savers to invest in another country. Third, by privatizing some of the loss-incurring public enterprises such as public transport and postal and telecommunication services, it has injected an element of efficiency into the running of public services. Fourth, by removing the obstacles to cross-border movement of productive resources, it has enabled the owners of such resources to earn income from countries outside their own. And, finally, the technological changes that expedited the process of

[1] For an interesting discussion of the rise and fall of the welfare state, see Mishra 1999.

globalization have benefited people by making transport and communication speedier, more comfortable, and less expensive.

Yet, behind this brighter side lies the darker side of globalization which is causing resentment worldwide but more bitterly from its direct victims. The victimized groups are too many to enumerate, and in sheer numbers they represent the majority of the world's population. The protest groups that gathered in Seattle in 1999 and later in Davos, Melbourne, and Prague to campaign against the pro-globalization policies of the International Monetary Fund (IMF) and the World Bank (WB) were only the most articulate of this vast population. In essence, the protest message was a simple one: the economic gap between the minority have-lots and the majority have-nots is widening, and globalization is accentuating this cleavage by promoting greed and venality in the name of self-interest and market competition.

Quoting from the *Human Development Report of 1996,* Martin and Schumann have shown that a total of 358 people own as much wealth as 2.5 billion people own together —nearly half of the world's population. Also, the wealthiest fifth of the world's nations dispose of 84.7 percent of the world's combined GNP; its citizens account for 84.2 percent of the world's trade, and possess 85.5 percent of savings in domestic accounts (Martin and Schumann 1997, 23 and 29). If one ranks the national economies and multinational corporations (MNCs) in terms of total output of the former and total sales of the latter, one would see that among the top one hundred in the list more than fifty will be MNCs.

Finally, while CEOs of private corporations enjoy six-digit annual salaries and other fringe benefits, the tragic fate of the more than 800 million unemployed and underemployed on the eve of the twenty-first century is a different story altogether. Adam Smith, realizing this sad potential of the free market wrote with perspicacity: "[A]ll for ourselves and nothing for other people, seems, in every age of the world, to have been the vile maxim of the masters of mankind" (Smith 1981, book III, 366). In short, the persistence and the widening of the "development gap" between the rich and the poor nations and between rich and poor people is an indication, as Arthur MacEwan concludes, that little has changed in the world since the dawn of the twentieth century

(MacEwan 1999, 1). This disparity is morally obscene, economically unjust, socially intolerable, and therefore politically perilous. Hence, the discontent against economic globalization and its underlying liberal philosophy. As Karl Polanyi said, "[T]o allow the market mechanism to be sole director of human beings and their natural environment . . . would result in the demolition of society" (Polanyi 1957, 73). Islam would agree with him.

THE ISLAMIC CHALLENGE

Islam is a global religion. It strives to establish a compassionate, just, and benevolent socioeconomic order, not simply for Muslims alone but for all of humanity. "Verily this is no less than a message to (all) the worlds" (Qur'an 81:27), and the Prophet Muhammad was sent "as a mercy to all creatures" (Qur'an 21:107) declares the Qur'an. Freedom, responsibility, and accountability are the essence of the Islamic Order. Allah (God of Islam) is One, and He is *rab al-a'lamin*, which means, the Cherisher and Sustainer of the worlds. Therefore, His message delivered to humankind through thousands of prophets[2] cannot be different to different societies.

Long before the current phase of global capitalism, religious and cultural forces held sway. Between the eighth and fourteenth centuries when much of Europe was still in the Dark Ages, Islam was at the forefront of a multi-ethnic, multiconfessional civilization that centered around the Mediterranean and the Silk Route. Ideas on science and technology and knowledge from the arts and humanities crossed geographical borders and cultural boundaries with as much ease as trade and commerce.

In this civilization, economics and economic development were subsumed under the paramount objective of human development, and that development was conditioned by the ethical and moral values of the religion. For example, production and profit were treated not as ends but means to the improvement of human welfare. In fact, the human social-welfare function as

[2] The Qur'an names dozens of prophets, including Abraham, David, Salih, Nuh, Lot, Jacob, Joseph, Moses, and Jesus, and concludes by saying that there is no nation in this world to whom Allah had not sent a prophet.

developed by Al-Ghazalli and later by Al-Shatibi, two of the hundreds of intellectual savants produced by medieval Islam, not only predates the current thinking on the subject by about eight hundred years but lies in sharp contrast to the ideas of neoclassical economists (Zarqa 1980, 3-18). Whereas modern economists consider the social-welfare function as the result of individual rational choices, Islamic thinkers viewed it as the product of religiously determined values. The qualities of benevolence, justice, moderation, humility, honesty, and forgiveness, which the Qur'an promotes, and greed and niggardliness, which it condemns, are the guiding principles of Islam that determine a society's welfare function. In short, Islam in its global mission had a holistic approach to human society in which economic growth and material advancement were only the means to an end and not the end in itself. This does not mean that there is no place for economic enterprise in Islam. It only means, as will be explained soon, that the goals of global capitalism and global Islam are incongruent.

To understand the Islamic perspective in relation to globalization and the global economy, one should start with a few of the fundamental tenets of Islamic philosophy. First, Islam denies the separation of the secular from the spiritual. Unlike Christianity, Islam never surrendered that which belonged to Caesar to Caesar. Instead Islam gave everything to God and allowed Caesar to enjoy only what God permitted him to enjoy, and that also within the guidelines set by God. In other words, as mentioned already, Islam takes a holistic approach to human life and problems, which means that no domain in life—be it political, economic, or even religious—can be treated in isolation with total disregard to the overall Islamic *Weltanschauung*, or "worldview."

Second, although "all things in the heavens and on earth" (Qu'ran 2:255) belong to God, human beings were created with God's spirit breathed into them (Qu'ran 15:29) as God's *khalifa*, or "vicegerents" on earth (Qu'ran 15:30; 6:165). They were given full freedom to choose between good and evil.[3] Third, without

[3] This freedom of choice was a "trust," or *amanah*, that, according to the Qur'an, man undertook while the earth and the mountains refused. See Qur'an 33:72.

leaving men and women entirely on their own, God in His infinite mercy decided to provide them with clear guidance periodically through his messengers, the Prophet Muhammad being the last of such messengers. Finally, there is accountability, reward, and punishment in the hereafter for all that people do in this world.

These fundamental tenets in Islam have important ramifications for the economic behavior of human beings and economic progress. Unlike in the case of economic liberalism, there is no place in Islam either for individual self-interest or for the market forces to enjoy unrestricted freedom. While, on the one hand, Islam exhorts a Muslim to be altruistic, responsible, fair, and productive, it emphasizes, on the other, the tragic consequences of breaking the ethical norms set by the Qur'an and the Prophet Muhammad. The concepts of *halal* ("that which is permitted") and *haram* ("that which is disallowed") and the fear of *akhira* ("the hereafter") permeate every action of the individual. As Timur Kuran writes, "The primary role of the [behavioral norms of Islam] is to make the individual member of Islamic society, *homo islamicus*, just, socially responsible, and altruistic. Unlike the incorrigibly selfish and acquisitive *homo economicus* of neoclassical economics, *homo islamicus* voluntarily forgoes temptations of immediate gain when by doing so he can protect and promote the interests of his fellows" (Kuran 1986, 135). Within the Islamic perspective, "scarcity is an unnatural condition caused by greed and avarice" (Warde 2000, 43). Even to a nonbeliever in Islam who looks at the economic problem objectively, scarcity is not absolute but relative to human demand. As Douglas Dowd makes clear, ". . . the reality is that resources are *not* scarce and human wants are *not* unlimited—except in the sense that resources are *made* to be scarce through some combination of frivolous and wasteful patterns of consumption and production, and that wants are *induced* through advertising to become unlimited" (Dowd 2000, 15). A Muslim believes that Allah is the provider, and there is plenty in this world for all to share, provided His creatures live by His commands.

The Qur'an provides explicit incentive for economic enterprise when it says, "When the call is proclaimed to prayer on Friday, hasten earnestly to the remembrance of God, and leave off business . . . and when the prayer is finished then may ye disperse through the land, and seek the Bounty of God" (Qu'ran 62:9-10). However, it warns against defrauding and committing excesses while seeking the bounty of God. "Give just measure and cause no loss by fraud and weigh with scales true and upright" (Qu'ran 26:181-82). Unlimited accumulation of wealth in the hands of a few to the detriment of many is condemned in the Qur'an. "Woe to (those) who pileth wealth and layeth it by, thinking that his wealth would make him last" (Qu'ran 104:1-3). "And there are those who bury gold and silver and spend it not in the way of God: announce to them a most grievous penalty" (Qu'ran 9:34). The duty of *zakat* ("obligatory charity") was specifically instituted in Islam in order to prevent this type of accumulation so that wealth "may not (merely) make a circuit between the wealthy" (Qu'ran 59:7). The Prophet Muhammad was also concerned that greed which leads to unlimited accumulation would erode a person's religious belief and lead him astray. "Two wolves let loose in a flock of sheep would do as much damage to it as greed for wealth and status would do to a man's faith," he said (Chapra 1970, 3-18). The story of Qarun (Korah) in the Qur'an, which explains how a fabulously wealthy person ruined himself and his people and through sheer arrogance revolted against the leadership of Moses and Aaron, amply illustrates this point.[4]

One of the distinct characteristics of the global economy is the massive increase in the size of the financial market. Trillions of dollars circulate around the world daily in search of higher returns in the form of interest payments, dividends, arbitrage, and capital gains. Only about one-fifth of this colossal amount is actually required to finance the production and exchange of real goods and services. This means nearly eighty percent of the money in circulation is "hot money," the lifeblood of "casino capitalism," whose sole purpose is to make even more money. "The world has become one large casino whose gambling tables are scattered from one end of the globe to the other" (Longworth 1998, 8). The rate of return to this finance capital is related to the risk involved so

[4] Qur'an 28:76. For the story of Korah in the Bible see Numbers 16.

that the greater the risk, the larger the return. The Islamic prohibition of *riba* ("usury") and its restrictions on *gharar* ("risk") strike at the very heart of this financial system. The term *riba*, as Ibrahim Warde explains, "is not necessarily about interest rates as such, and it certainly is not exclusively about interest rates. It really refers to any unlawful gain derived from the quantitative inequality of the countervalues *(inequality of exchange values in real terms)*. Interest or usury . . . would then be only one form of *riba*" (Warde 2000, 58). Similarly, *gharar*, a word that is mentioned in the *hadiths*[5] but not in the Qur'an, connotes deception or delusion, peril, risk, or hazard. Based on the analysis by Maxime Rodinson, Warde stresses that Islam without advocating the avoidance of risk in general prohibits only "aleatory *(i.e., subject to the influence of chance)* transactions . . . conditioned on uncertain events" (Warde 2000, 59). It is on this basis that Islam also prohibits *maysir* ("gambling"). In the context of the global financial market, these Islamic restrictions will significantly impinge on the operation of the short-term and speculative activities of fund managers, financiers, and their respective institutions. With excess capacity and dwindling rates of return to capital investment in the "real" economic sectors such as manufacturing and agriculture in the world economy, the capitalists are shifting their investment to more risky sectors such as the stock market. It is this sort of investment that has been the cause of numerous financial and economic crises since the 1970s. The Islamic system would severely restrict such speculative investments.

Islam is not against the profit motive, the cardinal principle of free-market ideology; but it is not willing to allow the profit motive to determine human progress. According to the free-market ideology, profit enables accumulation; accumulation leads to saving and investment; investment promotes economic growth; and economic growth bestows human prosperity and happiness. This "tunnel vision" of the free marketeers and their ideological supporters has produced misery and suffering to millions around

[5] *Hadiths* are the sayings of the Prophet Muhammad. Of the various compilations of *hadiths* the most famous is that of Al Bukhari (d. 870), which has 7,275 of the Prophet's sayings. The *hadith* literature is unique to Islam.

the world. This suffering is the cumulative result of a number of factors such as: (a) an increasing concentration of wealth in the hands of a few and the yawning gap between the rich and the poor; (b) the short-termism and speculation that dominate modern financial markets; (c) the reckless destruction to the environment caused by modern techniques of production; (d) the rising trend of consumerism; and, (e) the passionate obsession with economic growth. All these factors and the social disruption that they have engendered are areas of conflict between the Islamic economic perspective and the global economy.

The Ideal and the Reality

However, ideological Islam is different from Islam in practice. In spite of nearly thirty years of religious resurgence since the 1970s and a successful revolution in the name of Islam in Iran, nowhere in the Muslim world have the Islamic economic ideals been fully realized. Even in the field of political and economic literature, no work has yet been produced by the Islamists that could be called a blueprint for action. As Warde points out, "[Q]uantity, not quality, is the defining feature of writings on Islamic economics . . ." (Warde 2000, 9). Apart from a few ad hoc reforms introduced in some Muslim countries, specifically in the areas of taxation, banking, and finance, free-market ideology and economic liberalism dominate the world of Islam. Poverty, greed, consumerism, environmental destruction, and exploitation of the weak and the indigent are common in the Muslim countries, as they are in most parts of the world. Why has the Muslim world failed to realize the economic ideals of its religion?

The reasons for the failure are both external and internal to Islam. Externally, international power politics and disunity among the Muslim countries have left them with no alternative but to fall in line with the prevailing world order. Neither the Organization of the Islamic Conference (OIC) nor the Organization of Arab Petroleum Exporting Countries (OAPEC), the two most powerful Muslim organizations, have any political clout to influence international decisions. This aspect has been exhaustively dealt with in a number of studies in the field of international political economy.

Of more importance to the present discussion are the reasons internal to Islam. Islam has a comprehensive worldview that endeavors to answer all questions of human existence. In the medieval era, the Muslim jurists interpreted the two premier sources of the religion, the Qur'an and the *hadiths*, to derive a code of *shariah* ("religious laws") which answered almost all questions of that time. However, the changes that have taken place since the dawn of the twentieth century in practically every area of human life have been so dramatic that the traditional body of knowledge handed down by the medieval jurists requires substantial updating to meet the new challenges. There has, therefore, arisen a demand for the doors of *ijtihad* ("interpretation"—that is, using personal effort to derive a point of law), which had remained closed since the tenth century, to re-open. It is in updating the *shariah* to make it more applicable and relevant to modern life that the world of Islam is unable to reach a consensus.

The *shariah* simply means the Islamic moral and legal system. The principal sources of the *shariah* are the Qur'an and the *sunnah*. The *sunnah* consists of the sayings of the Prophet Muhammad and his actions or behavior. In addition to the principal sources there are two subsidiary sources: *ijma'*, the "consensus of the opinion of Muslim jurists," and *qiyas,* "reasoning by analogy."[6] Unlike in Catholicism where the pope can make a ruling which then becomes binding on the followers across the Catholic world, there is no supreme mufti in Islam whose *fatwas* ("religious rulings") bind every Muslim. Apart from the historic split between the *ulama* ("religious scholars") of the *shiah* and *sunni* schools, which bedevils religious coordination between Iran and the rest of the Muslim world, there is, in addition, a lack of unanimity in interpreting the Qur'an and *sunnah* within the *sunni ulama* themselves.[7]

This lack of unanimity in the interpretation of the *shariah* has had an impact on the Islamization of Muslim political, economic, and social life. While Muslim clerics and scholars remain divided

[6] For a brief explanation of these sources, see Esposito 1998, 68-114.

[7] Ibrahim Warde has devoted an entire chapter on the issues and controversies involved in interpreting the *shariah*. See Warde 2000, 226-37.

over matters of *shariah*, the Muslim governments and their ruling elite, who have vested interests in maintaining the status quo, have found it convenient to avoid any radical transformation of the system based on Islamic values. All that has been achieved so far in respect to Islamization can be reduced to a few measures instituted haphazardly in the fields of finance, taxation, and matters of civil life. The unwillingness of the Muslim rulers to undertake the necessary socioeconomic reforms based on the universal principles of Islam is a telling illustration of the failure of Islam in practice.

Another reason that is internal to the Muslim world is the conflicting approach to Islamization between the conservatives and modernists. Conservatives, like the members of the *Jamaat Tabligh*, a fluid organization born in the town of Mewat near Delhi in India as the brainchild of Maulana Ilyas (1885-1944) with a vast following all around the world, concentrate on Islamizing the individual and stress the importance of adhering to the five pillars of Islam: *shahada* ("proclamation of faith"); *salat* ("the five daily prayers"); *zakat* ("the obligatory wealth tax"); *saum* ("the fast during the Muslim month of Ramadan"); and *hajj* ("the pilgrimage to Mecca"). To conservatives, life in this world is transient and the less Muslims concentrate on *dunya* ("the affairs of this world"), the better their chance of success in *akhira* ("the hereafter").[8] A number of political, economic, and social issues that are dominating modern intellectual debate are outside their immediate concern. This unfortunate development has converted a substantial section of the Muslim population into a group of voluntary social masochists who would tolerate political, economic, and social injustices for the sake of the hereafter. "The poor and the meek shall inherit the Kingdom," stressed the Catholic Church in the eighteenth and early-nineteenth centuries when the working classes were protesting against the inequities of industrial capitalism. In a similar manner, the Muslim conservatives of the present

[8] For a brief description and analysis of the *Tabligh Jamaat*, see Mumtaz Ahmad, "Islamic Fundamentalism in South Asia: The Jamaat-I-Islami and Tablighi Jamaat," in *Fundamentalisms Observed*, ed. Martin E. Marty and R. Scott Appleby (Chicago and London: University of Chicago Press, 1991): 510-14.

day are appealing to their followers to shun this world so that they may succeed in the hereafter. To them, reforming or reinterpreting the *shariah* is unnecessary because the *imams* of the previous era have completed that job,[9] and all that is left for the Muslims to do is to follow the *shariah* as it is.

Modernists, however, who are mainly intellectuals and academics without an organization, stress the dynamic nature of Islam and the crucial mission of the human being in this world who, as God's *khalifa,* undertook the trust from God to implement His moral law (al-Faruqi 1998, 81-85). It is in the implementation of this moral law that Islam becomes relevant to the global economy. Political oppression, economic inequality, social discrimination, and religious bigotry are against the moral law of Islam, and modernists believe that it is the duty of every Muslim to join the forces that are trying to eliminate these evils. This radical and dynamic way of looking at Islam is a threat to the status quo and is bound to provoke resistance from a coalition of factions that have vested interest in the present order. The modernists are unfortunately a minority in the Muslim world. Their influence among the Muslim masses is therefore limited. The ideas of the Muslim modernists are often condemned as religious heresy by the ruling Muslim elite and its *ulama* supporters.

Of the reasons that are external to Islam, one needs mentioning at this juncture. It is the distorted image of Islam that is being propagated in the West. This distortion has a long history, beginning with the Crusades. However, in the present era some of the political developments in the Muslim world, such as the Arab-Israeli conflict, the Iranian Revolution, the Gulf War, and the political unrest in Algeria in combination with the Anglo-American and European economic interests in the Middle East, have accentuated the trend. As a result of this distortion some Western scholars like Samuel Huntington view Islam not only as a threat to Western civilization but also as a source of future conflict (Huntington 1993). In contrast, Islam is a fountain of redemption for a civilization in great economic sin.

[9] The most reputable of the *imams* in *Sunni* Islam are Abu Hanifa (c. 703-767), Malik (717-801), Shafii (769-820), and Ibn Hanbal (778-855).

Does this mean that the global economy cannot be reformed from an Islamic perspective? The Islamic values and its moral laws are universally valid. In fact, as al-Faruqi demonstrates in his penetrating analysis of Islam and other faiths, these values and morals are the universal property of every human being as part of the *din al-fitra* ("natural religion"). Whether the person is Muslim, Christian, Jew, Buddhist, Hindu, or atheist, that person has a right to God's moral law. Values and morals are not, therefore, the monopoly of Islam, and Muslims are duty-bound to support anyone or any group that is trying to give practical shape to these values and laws. The reshaping of the global economy to reflect God's moral law is a duty incumbent upon every concerned human being. The struggle against political oppression, economic deprivation, unlimited accumulation, and uncontrolled destruction of the environment is a universal struggle that has been sanctioned by Islam and championed by its Prophet. The protests against the global economy and globalization have emerged from a variety of groups such as the trade unionists, communists, feminists, environmentalists, and so on. Islam does not agree with some of the basic philosophies of these groups, but on the economic side of their protests Islam is a friend rather than a foe. There are a number of areas where the anti-globalizationists and Muslims can find agreement.

DISCUSSION QUESTIONS

1. Discuss briefly the economic principles of Islam, and relate them to the problems of the global economy.

2. Globalization and free markets are a recipe for political instability and social disharmony. Do you agree or disagree? State your reasons.

3. How does Islam categorize human actions? What are some of the practices in modern economies that may fall under these categories?

4. Discuss the Islamic view on interest. Can there be an interest-free economy? Why or why not?

5. On what grounds can Muslims find common ground with the aspirations of the anti-globalization movement?

SUGGESTED FURTHER READINGS

Ahmad, Khurshid. "Islam and the Challenge of Economic Development." In *The Challenge of Islam,* ed. Altaf Gauhar. London: Islamic Council of Europe, 1978.

Baqer Sadr, Muhammad, and Ayatullah Sayyid Mahmud Taleghni. *Islamic Economics: Contemporary Ulama Perspectives.* Kuala Lumpur: Iqra, 1991.

Engineer, Ashgar Ali. *Islam and Its Relevance to Our Age.* Bombay: Institute of Islamic Studies, 1984.

Lewis, Mervyn K., and Latifa M. Algaoud. *Islamic Banking.* Cheltenham, U.K.: Edward Elgar, 2001.

Rahman, Fazlur. *Major Themes of the Quran.* Chicago: Bibliotheca Islamica, 1980.

Thunderbird International Business Review 41, no. 4/5 (July-October 1999).

CONCLUSION

By Chandra Muzaffar

In their responses to the global economy, our seven contributors have chosen to focus upon two areas: one, some of the strengths, and to an even more significant degree, the severe shortcomings in the global economy; and two, those values, principles, and ideals embodied in each of their religions or moral philosophies which intimate a vision of life that in essence is different from what the current global system has to offer.

OVERVIEW

We shall first examine Igbo and African, Hindu, Buddhist, Confucian, Judaic, Christian, and Islamic perspectives on the global economy to get a sense of the commonalities in the positions they hold. Then an attempt will be made to elucidate the values, principles, and ideals articulated on behalf of each religion to discover their similarities. How these affinities can be developed through interreligious dialogue in order to evolve a shared universal spiritual and moral ethic to undergird the global economy is the next question that we shall address. This will take us to the challenge of translating such an ethic into tangible institutions and concrete policies. A case will then be made for adopting an action-oriented approach to articulating the alternative.

Whether the vested interests that preserve and perpetuate the present global system will allow an ethic that threatens their wealth and power to emerge and grow is yet another important issue that we will have to grapple with. We then argue that however formidable the obstacles, religions in pursuing their commitment to social justice and human dignity should never resort to means that undermine their own moral foundations. For in the ultimate analysis, it is apparent that the unjust global economy and the greed that is inherent in it can only be "subverted" through a profound spiritual transformation of the self.

GLOBAL ECONOMY: COMMONALITIES

Strengths

It is significant that a number of our contributors acknowledge that the global economy has succeeded in generating wealth which has brought some benefits to sections of the human family. It is through the creation of wealth that a nation is often able to provide basic amenities to the poor, educate the young, and look after the sick. Needless to say, each and everyone of these activities has much merit in the eyes of religion.

At the same time, the global economy—especially through the current phase of globalization—has made communication and transportation cheaper and more efficient. This has made it possible for millions of people to interact with one another across cultural borders and religious boundaries as never before in human history. Since the ideal of a universal human community lies at the heart of almost all spiritual traditions, this is yet another accomplishment of the global economy which religious men and women should applaud (Muzaffar 1998a).

Shortcomings

Nonetheless, for the religions as a whole, the shortcomings of the global economy overwhelm its few achievements. Not all these shortcomings are due entirely to the workings of the global economy per se. National elites and other forces within domestic economies are equally responsible for many of the ills that plague humanity.

Poverty remains a major global challenge. As almost every one of our contributors observes, the gap between the very rich and the very poor is increasing at an alarming rate. To put it in more graphic terms: "840 million people in our world—a number equal to the combined populations of Canada, the United States, Japan, and Europe—go to bed hungry every night. 1.3 billion people have to survive on earnings equivalent to less than US $1 a day. At the moment, the richest 20 percent of the world's population commands over 85 percent of its income and assets. An ordinary Sri Lankan worker would have to work for 1,200 years to earn the daily income of just one of the world's 350 richest billionaires. The annual average spent on a Norwegian pet cat is twice as much as most people in Sub-Saharan Africa earn in a year" (Tyndale 2001, 1). Add to all this yet another statistic, in 1960, "the 20 percent of the world's people who live in the richest countries had 30 times the income of the poorest 20 percent—by 1995 82 times as much income."[1]

Abject poverty and widening disparities in income are compounded by the chronic burden of debt, declining national revenues, and deteriorating terms of trade of a number of so-called developing countries. Nearly all the religious traditions represented in this study are of the view that the International Monetary Fund (IMF), the World Bank (WB), and the World Trade Organization (WTO) have failed to ameliorate the problems of the poor and disadvantaged. If anything, these institutions have made the situation worse for the poor.

Since our contributors are seeking to evaluate the global economy from a religious perspective, poverty and destitution for them are not just issues of economic deprivation and diminished social opportunities. Poverty is cruel because it repudiates one's dignity as a human being. Denied the basic necessities of life, the poor are often forced to wait for handouts, for the crumbs to fall from the banquet tables of the rich. In extreme cases, they are even compelled to surrender their self-respect in order to survive.

But it is not simply because of its adverse impact upon the dignity of the poor that the global economy is damned. Since the concentration of wealth in the hands of a few is the driving force behind the global economy, it has created serious dichotomies and cleavages between the haves and have-nots which have weakened fraternity and solidarity within the human family. These divisions are at the root of certain current conflicts and may well ignite many more conflagrations in the future.[2]

What is worse, social iniquities and disparities, which are not just global phenomena but are also reflected at regional, national,

[1] *Human Development Report 1998* (New York: United Nations Development Program [UNDP], 1998), 29.

[2] The dire consequences of the global divide between rich and poor are highlighted in South Commission Report 1990.

and local levels, have gradually eroded certain time-honored values that all religions cherish—values such as caring, giving, and sharing. The pursuit of wealth, in other words, has become such an obsession among both individuals and corporations that one has little concern for the well-being of one's neighbor. The dominant attitude that is emerging everywhere, shaped no doubt by the credo of the global economy, is that one looks after oneself regardless of what happens to others; one's own interests are paramount; it is private gain that counts, the public good is of little consequence.

It is this self-centered thrust of the global economy—the antithesis of religious values —which explains the rise of greed as a social malaise in the contemporary world. The contemporary world has legitimized, sanctified, and normalized greed as no other epoch before us has done.[3] The ability of a single individual to accumulate billions of dollars—when billions of other human beings are struggling to eke out a meager existence—is often celebrated in the media and, indeed, by all strata of society as an outstanding testimony to capitalist enterprise.[4] That there must be something fundamentally wrong with a system that can allow such vast inequities to perpetuate themselves is a thought that does not occur to most of us because we have come to accept the global economy as some sacrosanct edifice, somewhat like how medieval Europe viewed the powerful church with awe and wonder!

Perhaps there is no better illustration of how ingrained greed is within the global economy than what we find in the practices of financial markets and currency speculation. With the intensification of financial liberalization and deregulation, currency speculators can move from one market to another, switch from Japanese yen to French francs to American dollars in a few minutes "and end up with deals worth millions" in different places (Martin and Schumann 1997, 49). The whole idea is to make as much profit as possible at lightning speed from sheer speculation in currencies. By transforming money into a commodity of profit

[3] Greed has existed right through history. For a study of greed see Goldberg 1994.

[4] The legitimization of greed is discussed in Muzaffar 1991.

which enters and exits markets at will, the entire financial system has become highly volatile (Strange 1998 and 1997). It is because of this volatile capital that currencies have plunged, stock markets have collapsed, and economies have disintegrated, leaving in their trail millions of unemployed and impoverished people, as happened in East Asia in 1997 and 1998 (Muzaffar 1998b). This crisis showed how the greed of a handful of currency speculators could cause widespread human suffering, especially in developing economies.

If greed can have such a devastating impact upon people, it can also wreak havoc upon the natural environment. In pursuit of quick profits, corporations, big and small, in different parts of the world have, in the last one hundred years, engaged in indiscriminate logging, thus reducing forest cover; corporations have polluted rivers and oceans, poisoned the air, and threatened fish, insects, mammals, and birds with extinction. Even the lifestyles of the "haves" are contributing toward environmental degradation. The private car, for instance, is one of the main causes of greenhouse-gas emissions, which have resulted in global warming. There is demonstrable evidence that "since 1976 the earth has been warming at the rate of 4-5 degrees per century—a trend which is unprecedented in the last 1000 years" (Schor 2001, 56). This, and other trends appear to reinforce the argument that current elite lifestyles and consumption patterns are ecologically unsustainable. As a critic of the consumer culture puts it, "We are laying waste to the renewables, destroying delicate ecosystems, and jeopardizing the planet's ability to support life as we know it" (Schor 2001, 56).

Why is this happening? Why is there so much greed within the economy? Why is there such an obsession with maximizing profits and multiplying private gain? Our interlocutors from the different religious and philosophical traditions are agreed that the root cause of the malady is economic liberalism, with its emphasis upon the pursuit of unfettered self-interest now expressing itself as neoliberalism. This economic philosophy that defines global capitalism subscribes to the view that the private entrepreneur should not be impeded by state regulations or other restrictions and should have the full freedom to take advantage of the market and maximize his profits. Only in such a liberal, deregulated environment—for the private entrepreneur—will people prosper and society progress.

That is the commonly held point of view, but our interlocutors think otherwise. The balance sheet on the global economy, as we see in this study, seems to prove them right. The empirical evidence endorses the contention that the global economy has failed to live up to the values, principles, and ideals enshrined in the seven religious and philosophical traditions that constitute the substance of this book.

VALUES, PRINCIPLES, AND IDEALS

The question we should now ask is this: Do the religions offer an alternative to the present global economy? If by an alternative one means a complete economic system with a guiding philosophy, structures, modalities, and goals, no scripture has the answer. Some of our authors make this salient point.

However, all religions do propound values, principles, and ideals that one should uphold which have a direct or indirect bearing upon the economy. The basic needs of everyone—food, clothing, shelter, education, health, and one should perhaps add, sexual fulfillment and human security—should be taken care of. There should be equitable distribution of wealth and opportunities. Indeed, distributive justice, part and parcel of the religions' larger commitment to justice, is emphasized by each and every writer in this collection of essays.

Public welfare or the public good also figures prominently in this book. There is no need to point out that it takes precedence over private gain or individual self-interest. The importance accorded to the public good is a reflection of yet another related concept found in certain religious traditions: that the community is an organism characterized by an intimate internal unity. This concept is linked to the idea that the economy is God's "household," as our Christian contributor, Sallie McFague, describes it. And the household is not just made up of human beings but of the whole of creation, finding resonance in the notion of an all-encompassing, all-embracing unity rooted in the oneness of God. It is significant that religions which appear to be so different from one another, such as Hinduism and Islam, embody this philosophical principle of unity.

It is this principle of unity which demands that the human being maintains that delicate ecological balance upon which all life on our planet depends. What this means is that economic growth and development, from a religious point of view, should not threaten the sustainability of the planet. On the contrary, developmental planning which is conscious of environmental ethics will enhance the harmonious relations between the human being and the environment. Underlying this consciousness—and indeed the principle of unity itself—is a profound recognition of the interdependence and interconnectedness of not just all life forms but of all things. The Buddhist insight into this is captured by the religion's interlocutor David Loy and parallels similar ideas found in numerous indigenous traditions, including Igbo.

An economy that recognizes interdependence and interconnectedness as guiding principles will have to function on a basis that is very different from the present global system. Such an economy will have to seek inspiration from the Confucian maxim, "In order to establish ourselves, we must help others to establish themselves; in order to enlarge ourselves, we have to help others to enlarge themselves." This is an explicit acknowledgment of the importance of assisting others. Indeed, assisting others becomes the prerequisite for ensuring one's own well-being. It shows how we are all connected to, and dependent upon, one another.

Applied to the global economy, this way of thinking means that the rich should help the poor and the strong should extend a hand to the weak, for the sake of the former. Narrowly conceived self-interest and private gain pursued without any consideration for the well-being of others—essential attributes of neoliberalism—would have no place in the Confucian moral ethic. What is remarkable about this ethic is that it is "other serving" without denying the importance of serving oneself.

In a sense, this maxim of helping others in order to help oneself is integral to that Golden Rule of Life found in all the spiritual traditions: Do not do unto others what you would not want others to do unto you. Expressed positively, it asks us to do to others what we want others to do to us. It is a rule that should be applied not only to the global economy but also to global politics and global society in general. The quintessence of this rule is reciprocity. Reciprocity is a deeply cherished value, not just in Confucianism but also in a number of other religions, cultures, and indigenous traditions. As Ifi Amadiume points out, in Igbo and African traditions reciprocity is expressed in numerous proverbs and sayings.

Like reciprocity, restraint is another value embodied in all the religions and moral philosophies discussed in this book. It has tremendous significance for the global economy. One can argue for restraint and moderation in the consumption patterns and even in the lifestyles of the elites in both "developed" and "developing" countries. This is bound to have a salutary effect upon the allocation of resources and the production of goods and services in society. Restraint in one's attitude toward the environment will almost certainly result in less ecological damage. This in turn will have an impact upon the economy. This is why the philosophies of Buddhism and Christianity, like those of Hinduism and Islam, have always recognized restraint as a great virtue which is sometimes mirrored in religious practices like fasting.

There are of course other values which our interlocutors have elaborated upon in their essays. Caring, sharing, and giving, which we have referred to in another context, are fundamental to all our religions. The pivotal significance of justice in the value system of most traditions is worth stressing over and over again. Likewise, compassion is as much a defining characteristic of Jewish thought as it is of Buddhist philosophy and, indeed, of other religions.

It is apparent that there is a comprehensive spectrum of values, principles, and ideals, ranging from restraint and moderation, on the one hand, to justice and compassion, on the other, at the *sanctum sanctorum* (the holy of holies) of all our traditions. These values should constitute the ethical core of the global economy. For most of our traditions, though not all, the ultimate source of these values is God. It is because these values are founded in God that they acquire a certain transcendent power and potency. They are perceived as absolute and sacrosanct. For the believer, faith in God therefore becomes an essential condition for sustaining one's commitment to these values.

The role of the human being is to translate these divine values into living values. This is part of the human being's mission as God's trustee in Christianity or God's vicegerent in Islam. Transforming the global economy in accordance with spiritual and moral values rooted in God-consciousness becomes the human being's special responsibility at this critical juncture in history.

In working toward this transformation, the human being is advised to choose "the middle way" or "the middle path." The middle path avoids the extremes—the extremes of puritanical asceticism and opulent extravagance. It is significant that the idea of the middle path exists in one form or another in most of the religious and philosophical traditions. In Confucianism, for example, establishing an equilibrium is equivalent to seeking a middle path. For Buddhism, "the Middle Way discovered by the Tathgata (the Buddha) avoids both extremes, giving vision, giving knowledge, it leads to peace, to direct knowledge, to enlightenment, to Nibbana" (Thompson 2000, 88). A Judaic tradition says, "The divine religion does not urge us to lead an ascetic life, but guides us in the middle path, equidistant from the extremes of too much and too little" (Cohn-Sherbok 2000, 155). In Islam, it is the middle nation "justly balanced" that is worthy of emulation. As stated in the Holy Qu'ran, "Thus have We made you an Ummah [community] justly balanced, that ye might be witnesses over the nations, and the Apostle a witness over yourselves" (Al Baqarah: 143).

UNIVERSAL SPIRITUAL AND MORAL ETHIC

We have shown that the different religions and philosophies have much in common in the values, principles, and ideals that they espouse, especially in relation to the global economy and the challenges it poses. Indeed, the similarities in their positions are so overwhelming that one can talk with some confidence about the religions evolving a shared universal spiritual and moral ethic vis-à-vis the global economy. However, for such an ethic to evolve, we have to go beyond our present endeavor. What we have done so far is to encourage each tradition to critique the global economy. But these traditions have not, as yet, really dialogued with one another. It is this interreligious dialogue that should now start in earnest. A serious, sincere, sustained dialogue among the religious and moral philosophies represented in this study focused upon the global economy and specific aspects of it is, undoubtedly, one of the most urgent tasks facing us today.

In the dialogue we envisage, the shared spiritual and moral values we have discovered will be subjected to in-depth scrutiny. For instance, while justice for the marginalized and downtrodden is our common goal, what exactly does Buddhism or Christianity or Islam mean by justice? Are there shades of difference in the way in which Judaism and Hinduism view compassion? Is interconnectedness in Igbo the same as interconnectedness in Buddhism? Will a Confucian with his understanding of moderation be able to empathize with a Muslim with her understanding of moderation?

By analyzing and exploring the meaning of values and principles that they uphold in common, it is quite conceivable that the followers of the various traditions will realize that while there are many similarities, there may also be subtle, nuanced differences in the way in which certain ideas are understood. This should not worry us. Such differences, put in their proper perspective, could deepen our understanding of the religion of our dialogue partner and even contribute toward strengthening our shared universal spiritual and moral ethic.

Values and Institutions

Once we have developed a more profound appreciation of the shared values and principles of the different religions and philosophies in relation to the global economy, we should take a couple more steps forward. We should try to translate some of the values and principles in our universal moral ethic into institutions and policies. This is one of the most effective ways of buttressing and sustaining our universal ethic.

Throughout history religion has shaped institutions and policies established by the state, including those that pertain to the economy. This is true of all the traditions we have studied. Of course, the influence of organized religion upon public policies has waned considerably in most parts of the world in the face of the secularization of society of the last two centuries or so. Nonetheless, with the re-emergence of religion as a powerful social and political force in a number of countries, organized religion is beginning once again to have an impact upon the state and the public realm.

While it is not inconceivable that some of the non-Muslim traditions do exert some influence upon economic and other public policies and institutions, we shall confine our observations to Islam simply because it is the religion with which this writer is most familiar. Muslims, especially in countries where they constitute the majority, continue to endow land and property for the public weal. The practice of endowment (*waqf*) was an important means by which a certain degree of social justice was achieved in the old days. It not only served to check the concentration of wealth in the hands of a few but it also provided support and sustenance for the poor. The inheritance system (*faraid*) still in force in a number of Muslim states is yet another mechanism that helps to ensure distribution of wealth, guided by a notion of rights wedded to responsibilities. There is also the wealth tax (*zakat*), one of the pillars of the religion, whose primary purpose is to distribute the surplus from a person's wealth—after all his needs have been taken care of —for the well-being of the poor and needy.

In recent decades, some Muslim governments have gone further and attempted to implement one of the most fundamental injunctions in the Qu'ran: the prohibition of interest (*riba*) (Chapra 1985). *Riba* is regarded as an extreme form of exploitation which oppresses both the individual and the community. In order to overcome this, governments in Iran, Sudan, Pakistan, Indonesia, and Malaysia, among other countries, have established *riba*-free banking systems or Islamic banks.

These Islamic banks have not really succeeded in curbing exploitation or even in reducing the financial burdens of the poor. On the whole, the overall impact of Islamic institutions upon the economy remains rather limited.[5] There are perhaps two reasons to explain this.

- These institutions, whether it is the *zakat* or the *waqf*, have been grafted onto an economic system whose basic ideology and structures are alien to the Islamic value system and worldview. More specifically, since most Muslim economies are caught in the web of neoliberalism and crass capitalism, the Islamic institutions and practices appended to them have not been able to ameliorate problems of injustice and exploitation. In an increasingly globalized world, it is going to be even more difficult to develop autonomous economic systems which are not subservient to the dominant paradigm.
- Equally important, in many Muslim countries, most institutions of governance including Islamic economic agencies have failed miserably because of the venality or sheer incompetence, or both, of the elites themselves. Bereft of any commitment to the public good, they have often abused their wealth and power to the utter detriment of the poor.

In spite of the formidable odds facing Islam and other religions which are determined to create more just and equitable institutions at the national and global level, they should not waver in their resolve. For a start, in the endeavor to translate values and principles from a universal moral ethic into tangible institutions and concrete policies, the religions could address the following five challenges.

(1) *Wealth Distribution*

Is it possible to establish institutions at the global level to ensure that a significant portion of the vast wealth that has been generated in the last two or three decades is directed toward the eradication of global poverty? Would this require dismantling, or at least restructuring, some of the existing global institutions? Or,

[5] There is some evaluation of Islamic economic institutions and practices in *Review of Islamic Economics* 9 (Leicester: Islamic Foundation, 2000).

is this a goal that can only be accomplished after a massive transformation in the global power structure?

(2) *Corporate Wealth*

Is it possible to arrest the trend toward greater and greater concentration of wealth in the hands of a few megacorporations which are largely responsible for ever-widening global inequities? In this regard, can we establish alternatives to transnational corporations (TNCs), which, while retaining some of their advantages, will, at the same time, be more just and fair to the interests of the majority of humankind? Here again, are these changes that can only be achieved after the neoliberal capitalist ideology is laid to rest?

(3) *Consumer Culture*

Is it possible to curb the rampant global consumer culture? Apart from counseling restraint and moderation in the consumption patterns of elites and even urging them to lead by example, are there other changes that should be introduced? Should we be thinking of changing the motives, content, character, and aims of advertising since advertisements play such a big role in sustaining the consumer culture? Can we align advertising with religious values by making advertising much more ethical and socially responsible? Will such an attempt incur the wrath of the entire capitalist establishment, given the critical position that the advertising industry occupies in the edifice of wealth and power?

(4) *Money as a Commodity*

Is it possible to ensure that money is used only as a medium of exchange and is not abused as a commodity for profit? In order to curb and eliminate currency speculation altogether, what sort of mechanisms should be instituted at the global, regional, and national levels? Will currency dealers and financial markets that wield enormous power allow such mechanisms to be established? Or, will any attempt to overhaul the international financial architecture be crushed mercilessly by the rich and the powerful?

(5) *Stock Market Reforms*

Is it possible to develop an alternative stock market, minus speculative business instruments? Given the importance of the stock market in a modern economy, can it be reformed so that it retains its original functions of a meeting place for traders to exchange information and a place for genuine buying and selling of stocks and shares without getting involved in margin-selling, short-selling, and long-buying options and futures trading? Will there be tremendous resistance to such changes since speculative activity and market manipulation have become part and parcel of the stock market?

It is obvious that any serious, systematic attempt to introduce institutions or propose policies that reflect elements of our universal moral ethic will be met with strong opposition from those who want to preserve the status quo. Nonetheless, we should continue to formulate alternative ideas and institutions for the global economy since we have yet to give concrete expression to many of the values that we have been espousing on behalf of our respective religions. As we have shown, on issues such as alternatives to TNCs or new forms of advertising or a different conception of money or a nonspeculative stock market, we have not done much thinking. It is thinking at this level, guided by values and principles culled from our religions, that we should be actively engaged in.

Religious interlocutors and scholars alone will not be able to develop the concrete, tangible type of thinking that the situation demands. They will have to dialogue with economists, sociologists, development planners, and others who are better versed in the workings of the global economy. Together, they should produce alternative ideas that are not only bold and imaginative, but also feasible and practical.

ANOTHER STEP: ACTION

Concretizing and institutionalizing values and principles aside, there is another step forward that we should take. Those of us who are inspired by a shared universal spiritual and moral ethic should become more action oriented. An action-oriented approach could express itself in two ways: at the intellectual level and at the grassroots level.

The scholars who have spoken on behalf of the different religions and moral philosophies in this book have demonstrated the importance of responding to the challenge of the global economy through rigorous intellectual analysis and reflection. One hopes that many others will follow suit. As more and more religious voices speak up, the general public, if not the powers that be, will take note.

The public will become aware of the arguments that these voices are making, and why their arguments are different from what others are saying if, at the same time, they are articulated through the mainstream media. Whenever there is an issue in the public arena—it may be the WTO's new trade rules or some IMF diktat or some TNC's foul-up—individuals and groups operating from within a religious perspective should take a stand. Every time the United Nations Development Program (UNDP) produces its annual *Human Development Report,* the advocates of a universal ethic should respond. And we reiterate: they should make their views known through the mainstream media.

It is a pity that sane, rational, well-argued religious perspectives on current, controversial economic issues, whether global or national, are not heard very often. This is why the public at large is not aware of the stand of the Dalai Lama or Desmond Tutu on an issue of paramount contemporary significance such as globalization. Unfortunately, sometimes a bigot on the fringes of a particular religion holds forth on some major controversy and gives a totally misleading picture of what his faith stands for. This is yet another reason why those who subscribe to a universal, inclusive, compassionate, humane view of religion and the human condition should be more vocal and more forthcoming.

At the same time, religious individuals and groups should, if circumstances permit, work among grassroots communities. Since there are a number of grassroots communities in the Philippines, Thailand, India, South Korea, and western Europe which are concerned about issues related to the global economy such as poverty, Third-World debt, the IMF's Structural Adjustment Programs

(SAPs), World Bank projects, the WTO's agenda, intellectual property rights, TNC operations, labor standards, and global warming, and are actively campaigning on these issues, there is no reason why religious individuals and groups cannot join hands with them. Of course, the leaders of many of these communities are secular in their orientation; but because the causes that they champion are also important to those with a religious background, the latter would be able to work with them on a common platform. Besides, religious individuals should see their participation as an opportunity to infuse these grassroots struggles with a universal spiritual and moral perspective which may well provide the social movements with much needed ballast.

Who's Paying Heed?

Are the rich and powerful paying heed to all these efforts by the little women and men of this planet? Are they listening to the voices from below, to the voices of the interlocutors of a spiritual moral ethic? Are they willing to respond?

The movers and shakers of the global economy know that there is a religious resurgence in many parts of the world and that they cannot afford to ignore the impact of religion upon society.[6] Religious sentiments are now accorded some consideration in the formulation of economic strategies. Both governments charged with managing the economy and the captains of industry concede that a pure secular outlook does not serve their own interests anymore.

Even international institutions that preside over the global economy have begun to acknowledge "the importance of spiritual and cultural life" ("World Faiths" 1998). As a case in point, the World Bank held a dialogue with the world's religious faiths in London in 1998 with the aim of promoting "better understanding between development agencies and the world faiths in defining and delivering development programs" (ibid.). While the holding of a dialogue is commendable, the World Bank, it appears, is not really prepared to come to grips with some of the fundamental issues raised by the world's religions, issues that

[6] This is acknowledged in the context of politics and international relations in Johnston and Sampson 1994.

reflect their worldviews which are at variance with the Bank's approach to development. This then is the critical point.

International institutions, together with the other institutions and elites that dominate the global economy, will make minor concessions here and there. They may try to preserve the traditional lifestyle of, say, an indigenous community affected by the construction of a megadam; or they may provide a bit of debt relief to some impoverished sub-Saharan state; or they may take steps to ensure that the fast food sold by some TNC conforms to the dietary rules of a religious community somewhere in Asia. But on issues that are vital to their power and control, the elites who rule the world will not concede an inch. These include a range of important possibilities such as diverting huge global resources toward the alleviation of mass poverty; or curbing the mammoth profits of the TNCs; or facilitating the growth of manufacturing industries in developing countries by not forcing them prematurely to compete on unfair terms with established firms in developed countries; or providing the developing world with easy access to scientific and technological knowledge in the developed world.

Right through this chapter we have made numerous references to the awesome power of those who are at the commanding heights of the global economy. Let us reinforce our thesis by highlighting the fact that a coterie of currency dealers determine global financial transactions; that a few hundred TNCs dominate global trade and industry; that a handful of megacorporations control the flow of news and the global entertainment culture; that a small number of first-class research centers dictate the scientific and technological agenda of the world (Korten 1995). The dominance of the powerful spans the globe. With elites in the North linked to elites in the South, with elites in the West connected to elites in the East, what has emerged in the last two decades is an extensive global network of power and wealth that has no particular home. Of course, in certain spheres of power, such as global politics and global security, it is Washington that calls the shots.

Because this network of power is so ubiquitous, it has come to be accepted as normal, even natural. It is not seen as dominance or control by most people. Whatever iniquities and injustices that exist are cleverly camouflaged from public scrutiny by the global media. Since the global economy, as we have seen, has brought some prosperity to certain sections of the human family, it is presented, and often applauded by the general public itself, as an outstanding success story. Besides, the culture of this success story—again projected by the media and the entertainment industry—is deceptively seductive. It is portrayed as a culture of fun and freedom which, willy-nilly, brings glitter and glory to all![8]

Transformation of the Self

The religions of the world must realize that resisting the power of a global economy wedded to such a seductive culture is a Herculean task. Resistance could lead to a great deal of frustration. It could even drive the advocates of change to despair. One can sense this in the protests of the anti-globalization movement which began in Seattle at the end of 1999 and have continued from city to city culminating in the violent demonstration in Genoa in the middle of 2001. The escalation of anger among the protesters was caused partly by the reluctance of the global economic and political elites to engage the anti-globalization movement in honest, sincere dialogue. The protesters, many of them young women and men, see very little hope for genuine change—change that will lead to a just world.

Religious groups and individuals have not figured prominently in the street protests of the anti-globalization movement. There is no evidence of rising anger or despair among religious groups opposed to globalization and injustice in the present global economy. Though an attempt was made by Osama bin Laden to link the September 11 attacks on the Pentagon and the World Trade Center in New York to the United States' global economic power[9]—as an afterthought—the indications are that the attacks were fueled by unhappiness and anger over U.S. foreign policy in the Middle East.

[8] Some of the cultural characteristics of capitalism are studied in Bell 1978.

[9] See his interview in *The Independent* (London), November 10, 2001.

For those of us who derive our strength and our vision from religion, the mode of engagement in our struggle against the injustices of the global economy is unambiguously clear. We eschew violence. We are committed to a peaceful, nonviolent quest for a just global economy. It is important to emphasize this because our struggle has a spiritual foundation. In all of our religious and philosophical traditions, it is lucidly stated that one should never separate means from ends. Since our end is noble—justice—we should use noble means to achieve it.

There is perhaps a more important reason why we should adhere to the right means. All said and done, our struggle is not just to change global structures, but also to check some of the underlying attitudes that sustain the global economy. Self-centeredness and greed have to be fought through nonviolent ways. Economic transformation, social education, and the building of awareness are some of the means we should employ. Most of all, it is through spiritual self-realization that one curbs and even eliminates vices such as greed. In every religion, the transformation of the self is one of the most sublime goals of life. It is the alpha and omega of change.

This is why the Buddha had stressed, "Though one should conquer a million men in battle yet he, indeed, is the noblest victor who has conquered himself" (Thera 1954, 97). Or, in the words of Jesus Christ, "What gain, then, is it for anyone to win the whole world and forfeit his life?" (Mark 8:36). Or, as the Prophet Muhammad put it, "The Mujahid (one who carries out *jihad*) is he who strives against himself for the sake of God" (Saifuddeen and Salleh 2001).

A simple, shared spiritual truth is found in every religion. It is this truth that is the essence of the response of the religions to the global economy. If greed can only be eliminated through conquest of self, and greed is at the root of the global economy, it follows that it is through the conquest of the self that the global economy will, in the end, rid itself of greed.

Works Cited

Abramowitz, Jane N. 1997. "Valuing Nature's Services," In *State of the World 1997*, ed. Lester R. Brown et al. New York: W. W. Norton, pp. 95-114.

Al-Faruqi, Ismail Raji. 1998. *Islam and Other Faiths*, ed. Ataullah Siddiqi. Leicester, U.K: Islamic Foundation.

Ali, A. Yusuf, translator. 1993. *The Holy Qu'ran*. Durban, South Africa: Islamic Propagation Centre International.

———. 1994. *The Holy Qu'ran*. Kuala Lumpur: Islamic Book Trust.

Amadiume, Ifi. 1987. *Male Daughters, Female Husbands: Gender and Sex in an African Society*. London: Zed Books.

———. 1995. "The Igbo and Ibibio." In *Encyclopedia of World Cultures*, volume 9, *Africa and the Middle East*, ed. John H. Middleton and Amal Rassam. New York: G. K. Hall/Macmillan.

———. 1997. *Reinventing Africa: Matriarchy, Religion and Culture*. London and New York: Zed Books.

Amadiume, Solomon. 1995. Translation, "Suitable Proverbs for Different Occasions: Similarities Between Igbo and Yoruba Proverbs." In *Ilu Ndi Igbo: A Study of Igbo Proverbs,* vol 2. Enugu, Nigeria: Fourth Dimension Publishing.

———. 1994. Translation, "Explanation and Usage: With a Comparison with Some Hausa Proverbs." In *Ilu Ndi Igbo: A Study of Igbo Proverbs,* vol. 1. Enugu, Nigeria: Fourth Dimension Publishing.

Aniakor, Chike C., and Herbert Cole. 1984. *Igbo Arts: Community and Cosmos*. Foreword by Chinua Achebe with contributions by Alexander Okwudor Attah et al. Los Angeles: University of California, Museum of Cultural History.

Annan, Kofi. 1999. "Role of the United Nations in Promoting Development in the Context of Globalization and Interdependence." United Nations publication. http://www.un.org/esa/ coordination/ ecosoc/revglobal.htm

Armstrong, R. G. 1982. "Is Earth Senior to God? An Old West African Theological Controversy." *African Notes* 9/1: 7-14.

Ban Gu. 1962. *Han shu: The Historiography of the Han*. Beijing: Zhonghua shuju.

Baran, Paul A., and P. M. Sweezy. 1968. *Monopoly Capital*. Harmondsworth: Penguin.

Bascom, William. 1972. "African Dilemma Tales: An Introduction." In

African Folklore, ed. Richard Dorson. Bloomington and London: Indiana University Press, pp. 143-55.

Bauman, Zygmunt. 1998. *Globalization: The Human Consequences.* Cambridge, U.K.: Polity Press.

———. 2000. *Liquid Modernity.* Malden, Mass.: Blackwell Publishers.

Beck, Ulrich. 2000. *What Is Globalization?* Malden, Mass.: Blackwell Publishers.

Beidelman, Thomas O. 1961. "Hyena and Rabbit: A Kaguru Representation of Matrilineal Relations." *Africa* 31:89-118.

———. 1963. "Further Adventures of Hyena and Rabbit: The Folktale as a Sociological Model." *Africa*: 33:54-69.

Bell, Daniel. 1978. *The Cultural Contradictions of Capitalism.* New York: Basic Books.

Bin Laden, Osama. 2001. Interviewed in *The Independent* [London], November 10, 2001.

Bloch, Maurice. 1971. *Placing the Dead: Tombs, Ancestral Villages and Kinship Organization in Madagascar.* London and New York: Seminar Press.

Bonhoeffer, Dietrich. 1960. *Letters and Papers from Prison.* London: Collins.

Borg, Marcus J. 1994. *Jesus in Contemporary Scholarship.* Valley Forge, Pa.: Trinity Press International.

Brown, Lester A., et al. *State of the World Annual Reports.* New York: W. W. Norton (issued annually).

Brutus, Dennis. 2000. "Africa 2000: In the New Global Context." In *African Visions: Literary Images, Political Change, and Social Struggle in Contemporary Africa,* ed. Cheryl B. Mwaria, Silvia Federici, and Joseph McLaren. Westport, Conn., and London: Praeger, pp. 3-6.

Caffentzis, George C. "The International Intellectual Property Regime and the Enclosure of African Knowledge." In *African Visions: Literary Images, Political Change, and Social Struggle in Contemporary Africa,* ed. Cheryl B. Mwaria, Silvia Federici, and Joseph McLaren. Westport, Conn., and London: Praeger, pp. 7-14.

Calame-Griaule, G. 1961. "L'Homme-Hyène dans la Tradition Soudanaise." *L'Homme* 1:89-118.

Chambers, Robert. 1997. *Whose Reality Counts?* London: Intermediate Technology.

Chapra, M. Umer. 1970. "The Economic System in Islam." *Islamic Quarterly* 14, no. 1: 3-18.

———. 1985. *Towards a Just Monetary System.* Leicester, U.K.: Islamic Foundation.

———. 1992. *Islam and the Economic Challenge.* Leicester, U.K.: Islamic Foundation; Herndon, Va.: International Institute of Islamic Thought.

Chavel, Charles B. 1980. *Encyclopedia of Torah Thoughts.* New York: Shilo Publishing House.

Chen Hui. 2001. Report from a conference on the travel industry held in Guangdong Province, China. *Nanfang dushi bao.* Guangdong (March 3, 2001).

Cohn-Sherbok, Dan, compiler. 2000. *The Wisdom of Judaism.* Oxford: Oneworld Publications.

Confucius. *The Analects (Lun yu),* translated with an introduction by D. C. Lau. New York: Penguin Books.

Costanza, Robert, et al. 1997. *An Introduction to Ecological Economics.* Boca Raton, Fla.: St. Lucie Press.

Crocker, David, and Toby Linden, eds. 1998. *Ethics of Consumption: The Good Life, Justice, and Global Stewardship.* Lanham, Md.: Rowman & Littlefield.

Cronbach, Abraham. 1949. "Social Thinking in the Sefer Hasidim." In *Hebrew Union College Annual* 22:1-147.

Crossan, John Dominic. 1994. *Jesus: A Revolutionary Biography.* San Francisco: HarperSan Francisco.

Daly, Herman E., and John B. Cobb, Jr. 1994. *For the Common Good: Redirecting the Economy Toward Community, the Environment, and a Sustainable Future.* 2nd ed. Boston: Beacon Press.

Daly, Herman E. 1996. *Beyond Growth: The Economics of Sustainable Development.* Boston: Beacon Press.

de Mahieu, Wauthier. 1985. "Towards a Semantic Approach to the Principle of Transformation: An Analysis of Two Myths Concerning the Origin of Circumcision among the Komo of Zaire." In *Theoretical Explorations in African Religion,* ed. Wim van Binsbergen and Matthew Schoffeleers. London and Boston: KPI, pp. 84-100.

Dollar, David, and Aart Kraay. 2000. "Growth Is Good for the Poor." Report of the World Bank Development of Research Group. http//www.worldbank.org/research/growth/pdfile/ growthgoodforpoor.pdf

Dowd, Douglas. 2000. *Capitalism and Its Economics.* London and Stirling, Va.: Pluto Press.

Durning, Alan. 1992. *How Much Is Enough?* New York: Norton.

Esposito, John L. 1998. *Islam: The Straight Path.* 3rd ed. New York: Oxford University Press.

Fanon, Frantz. 1963. *The Wretched of the Earth.* New York: Grove Press.

Federici, Silvia. 2000. "The New African Student Movement." In *African Visions: Literary Images, Political Change, and Social Struggle in Contemporary Africa*, ed. Cheryl B. Mwaria, Silvia Federici, and Joseph McLaren. Westport, Conn., and London: Praeger, pp. 49-66.

Fox, M., ed. 1975. *Modern Jewish Ethics*. Columbus: Ohio State University Press.

Freehof, Solomon B. 1959. *The Responsa Literature*. Philadelphia: Jewish Publication Society of America.

Friedman, Milton. 1953. *Essays in Positive Economics*. Chicago: University of Chicago Press.

Galbraith, John Kenneth. 1987. *A History of Economics*. London: Hamish Hamilton.

Geschiere, Peter. 1992. "Kinship, Witchcraft and the Market." In *Contesting Markets: Analyses of Ideology, Discourse and Practice,* ed. Roy Dilley. Edinburgh: Edinburgh University Press, pp. 159-79.

Goldberg, M. Hirsh. 1994. *The Complete Book of Greed.* New York: William Morrow & Company.

Goodwin, Neva R., Frank Ackerman, and David Kirion, eds. 1997. *The Consumer Society*. Washington, D.C.: Island Press.

Hackett, Steven C. 1998. *Environmental and Natural Resources Economics: Theory, Policy and the Sustainable Society*. Armonk, N.Y.: M. E. Sharpe.

Haney, Daniel Q. 2001a. "High HIV Rate in Gay Black Men." *Valley News,* October 6, 2001, B:1.

———. 2001b. "Government Aims to 'Break' AIDS Back." *Valley News,* February 7, B:1.

Hanh, Thich Nhat. 1988. *The Heart of Understanding*. Berkeley, Calif.: Parallax Press.

He Qinglian. 1998. *Xiandaihua de xianjing* (Traps of Modernization). Jinri zhongguo chubanshe.

Hendry, George. 1980. *Theology of Nature*. Philadelphia: Westminster.

Hirji, Karim F. 2000. "Academic Pursuits under the Links." In *African Visions: Literary Images, Political Change, and Social Struggle in Contemporary Africa*, ed. Cheryl B. Mwaria, Silvia Federici, and Joseph McLaren. Westport, Conn., and London: Praeger, pp. 67-84.

Huntington, Samuel. 1993. "The Clash of Civilization." *Foreign Affairs* 72, no. 3, pp. 22-44.

Isichei, Elizabeth. 1978. *Igbo Worlds: An Anthology of Oral Histories and Historical Descriptions*. Philadelphia: Institute for the Study of Human Issues.

Johnston, Douglas, and Cynthia Sampson, eds. 1994. *Religion, the Missing Dimension of Statecraft*. New York: Oxford University Press.

Korten, David C. 1995. *When Corporations Rule the World*. West Hartford, Conn.: Kumarian Press.

Kuran, Timur. 1986. "The Economic System in Contemporary Islamic Thought: Interpretation and Assessment." *International Journal of Middle East Studies* 18: 135-64.

Kurshid, Ahmad, ed. 1980. *Studies in Islamic Economics*. Leicester, U.K.: Islamic Foundation.

Lardy, Nicholas. R. 1999a. "China's Breathtaking WTO Offer Still Faces Significant Challenges." *Asian Wall Street Journal* (April 19, 1999): 10.

———. 1999b. "China's WTO Membership." Brookings Policy Brief #47 (April 1999). Available at http://www.brook.edu/dybdocroot/comm/policybriefs/pb047/pb47/htm.

Levathes, Louise. 1994. *When China Ruled the Seas: The Treasure Fleet of the Dragon Throne 1405-1433*. New York: Simon & Schuster.

Longworth, Richard C. 1998. *Global Squeeze: The Coming Crisis for First-World Nations*. New York: McGraw-Hill.

Loy, David R. 2000. "The Religion of the Market." In *Visions of a New Earth: Religious Perspectives on Population, Consumption, and Ecology*, ed. Harold Coward and Daniel C. Maguire. Albany: State University of New York Press, pp. 15-28.

Luttwak, Edward. 1999. *Turbo Capitalism*. London: Orion Business Books.

Luzzatto, Moshe Hayyim. 1987. *The Path of the Just*. New York: Feldheim Publishers. 2nd ed., chapter 11, trans. Shraga Silverstein.

MacEwan, Arthur. 1999. *Neo-Liberalism or Democracy? Economic Strategy, Markets, and Alternatives for the 21st Century*. London and New York: Zed Books.

Maimonides, Moses. 1963. *The Guide of the Perplexed*, trans. Shlomo Pines. Chicago and London: University of Chicago Press.

Martin, Hans-Peter, and Harald Schumann. 1997. *The Global Trap: Globalization and the Assault on Prosperity and Democracy*. London and New York: Zed Books.

Marshall-Fratani, Ruth. 1998. "Mediating the Global and Local in Nigerian Pentecostalism." *Journal of Religion in Africa* 28 (March 1998): 278-315.

Mencius. *The Works of Mencius*, trans. Jame Legge. New York: Dover Publications, and Hong Kong: The Chinese Book Co.

Meyer, Birgit. 1995. "'Delivered from the Powers of Darkness.' Confessions about Satanic Riches in Christian Ghana." *Africa* 65 (February 1995): 236-55.

Mishra, Ramesh. 1999. *Globalization and the Welfare State*. Cheltenham, U.K.: Edward Elgar Publishing.

Muzaffar, Chandra. 1991. "Towards a Spiritual Vision of the Human Being." In *The Human Being: Perspectives from Different Spiritual Traditions*. Penang: Aliran, pp. 199-219.

———. 1998a. "Globalisation and Religion: Some Reflections." In *Globalisation: The Perspectives and Experiences of the Religious Traditions of Asia Pacific*, ed. Joseph A. Camilleri and Chandra Muzaffar. Petaling Jaya: International Movement for a Just World, pp. 179-90.

———. 1998b. "Currency Speculation: A Global Virus." *Impact Magazine* [Manila] 33, no. 3: 10-12.

Mwaria, Cheryl B., Silvia Federici, and Joseph McLaren, eds. 2000. *African Visions: Literary Images, Political Change, and Social Struggle in Contemporary Africa*. Westport, Conn., and London: Praeger.

Ngolet, François. 2000. "Democratization and Interventionism in Francophone Sub-Saharan Africa." In *African Visions: Literary Images, Political Change, and Social Struggle in Contemporary Africa*. Westport, Conn., and London: Praeger, pp. 85-104.

Nienhaus, Voker. 2000. "Islamic Economics: Dogma or Science?" In *The Islamic World and the West,* ed. Kai Hafez. Leiden, Boston, and Cologne: Brill, pp. 86-99.

Payutto, P. A. 1994. *Buddhist Economics: A Middle Way for the Market Place,* trans. Dhammavijaya and Bruce Evans. 2nd ed. Bangkok: Buddhadhamma Foundation.

Polanyi, Karl. 1957. *The Great Transformation.* Boston: Beacon Press.

Rahman, Fazlur. 1979. *Islam*. 2nd ed. Chicago and London: University of Chicago Press.

Rasmussen, Larry L. 1996. *Earth Community Earth Ethics*. Maryknoll, N.Y.: Orbis Books.

Ricardo, David. 1993.*The Principles of Political Economy and Taxation*. London: Dent.

Rieger, Joerg, ed. 1998. *Liberating the Future: God, Mammon, and Theology*. Minneapolis: Fortress Press.

Rosen, Daniel. H. 1999. "China and the World Trade Organization: An Economic Balance Sheet." Also available online: http://www.chinaonline.com/commentary_analysis/d_rosen/ca_990707_ rosen_pg1.asp.

Ross, Robert R. J., and Kent C. Trachte. 1990. *Global Capitalism: The New Leviathan*. Albany: State University of New York Press.

Saifuddeen, Shaikh Mohd, and Shaikh Mohd Salleh. 2001. "Jihad does not mean holy war." *The Star* [Kuala Lumpur], October 12, 2001: 18.

Scholte, Jan Aart. 2000. *Globalization: A Critical Introduction*. London: Macmillan.

Schor, Julie. 2001. "Towards a New Politics of Consumption." In *Economics for Human Well-Being: Advancing a People's Agenda*. Cambridge, Mass.: Boston Research Center for the 21st Century. Keynote address at conference entitled "Beyond American Consumerism: Constructing a Transformative Politics," March 10, 2001, pp. 54-73.

Self, Peter. 2000. *Rolling Back the Market*. London: Macmillan.

Sizemore, Russell F., and Donald K. Swearer, eds. 1990. *Ethics, Wealth and Salvation: A Study in Buddhist Social Ethics*. Columbia, S.C.: University of South Carolina Press.

Smith, Adam. 1981. *The Wealth of Nations*. London: Everyman's Library.

———. 1950. *An Inquiry into the Nature and Causes of the Wealth of Nations*, vol. II. London: Methuen.

South Commission Report. 1990. *The Challenge to the South*. London: Oxford University Press.

Staudt, Kathleen. 1995. "The Impact of Development Policies on Women." In *African Women South of the Sahara*, ed. Margaret Jean Hay and Sharon Stichter. 2nd ed. London and New York: Longman, pp. 225-38.

Strange, Susan. 1997. *Casino Capitalism*. Manchester, U.K.: Manchester University Press.

———. 1998. *Mad Money: When Markets Outgrow Governments*. Ann Arbor: University of Michigan Press.

Su Xiaokang, and Wang Luxiang. 1991. *Deathsong of the River: A Reader's Guide to the Chinese TV Series Heshang*. New York: East Asia Program, Cornell University.

Tamari, M. 1987. *With All Your Possessions*. New York: Macmillan, Free Press.

Thompson, Mel, compiler. 2000. *The Wisdom of Buddhism*. Oxford: Oneworld Publications.

Thera, Narada, trans. 1954. *The Dhammapada*. London: J. Murray.

Tu Weiming. 1985. *Confucian Thought: Selfhood as Creative Transformation*. SUNY Series in Philosophy. Albany: State University of New York Press.

———. 1994. "Beyond the Enlightenment Mentality." In *Worldviews and Ecology: Religion, Philosophy, and the Environment,* ed. Mary Evelyn Tucker and John Grim. Maryknoll, N.Y.: Orbis Books, pp. 19-29.

Twersky, Isadore. 1982. "Some Aspects of the Jewish Attitude Toward the Welfare State." In I. Twersky, *Studies in Jewish Law and Philosophy.* New York: Ktav.

Tyndale, Wendy. 2001. "Towards Sustainable Development: A Shift in Values." *Commentary* 1, no. 8, August 2001. Petaling Jaya: International Movement for a Just World.

United Nations. *Annual UN Human Development Report (UNHDR).* New York: Oxford University Press. Also available online: http://www.undp.org/hdro/overview/pdf

van Binsbergen, Wim, and Matthew Schoffeleers. 1985. "Introduction: Theoretical Explorations in African Religion." In *Theoretical Explorations in African Religion,* ed. Wim van Binsbergen and Matthew Schoffeleers. London and Boston: KPI, pp. 1-49.

Walshe, Maurice, trans. 1995. *The Long Discourses of the Buddha: A Translation of the Digha Nikaya.* Boston: Wisdom Publications.

Warde, Ibrahim. 2000. *Islamic Finance in the Global Economy.* Edinburgh: Edinburgh University Press.

Waters, Malcolm. 1996. *Globalization.* London and New York: Routledge.

White, Lynn, Jr. 1967. "The Historical Roots of Our Ecological Crisis." *Science* 155 (March 10): 1203-7.

"World Faiths and Development Dialogue." 1998. Closing Statement by the Co-chairs. London: Lambeth Palace, February 18-19, 1998.

Zahan, Dominique. 1979. *The Religion, Spirituality, and Thought of Traditional Africa.* Chicago: University of Chicago Press.

Zarqa, Anas. 1980. "Islamic Economics: An Approach to Human Welfare." In *Studies in Islamic Economics,* ed. Kurshid Ahmad. Leicester, U.K.: Islamic Foundation, pp. 3-18.

Zhong Wei. 2001. "Zhongguo de shouru bujun you duo yanzhong?" Lianhe zaobao (Associated Morning Newspaper). Singapore (May 11, 2001): 17.

Zipperstein, Edward. 1983. *Business Ethics in Jewish Law.* New York: Ktav.

Zweig, Michael, ed. 1991. *Religion and Economic Justice.* Philadelphia: Temple University Press.

CONTRIBUTORS

Swami Agnivesh serves as chair of the United Nations Trust Fund on Contemporary Forms of Slavery and the Bandhua Mukti Morcha (Bonded Labor Liberation Front). The struggle against bonded labor and child labor has been at the heart of his activities to advance social and economic justice. He has led the movement toward liberation of bonded labor and child labor throughout India, been active in a range of women's issues, and conducted extensive tours throughout the country to promote self-confidence and awareness among the most vulnerable sections of Indian society. He is the author of numerous articles and the former chief editor of the biweekly *Rajdharma* (1968-1978). His most recent book is entitled *Religion, Spirituality, Social Action: A New Agenda for Humanity.*

Ameer Ali is lecturer in economics at the University of Western Australia. He taught at the University of Ceylon, Murdoch University, and at the University of Brunei Darussalam before coming to the University of Western Australia. He specializes in the development issues of Muslim countries. His monograph *From Penury to Plenty: Development of Oil Rich Brunei, 1906 to the Present* was published in 1996. He has published a number of articles in international journals including the *Journal of Interdisciplinary Economics*, the *Journal of Muslim Minority Affairs*, the *American Journal of Islamic Social Sciences*, and the *Journal of Objective Studies and South Asia.*

Ifi Amadiume is professor of religion and holds a joint appointment in the Department of Religion and the African-American Studies Program at Dartmouth College. She teaches courses on indigenous religions of Africa and women in African religions. She also teaches courses in African studies and women's studies. Born in Nigeria of Igbo parents, Professor Amadiume was educated in Nigeria and Britain and holds a Ph.D. from the University of London in social anthropology. She has done field work in Africa and has written several books, with a special interest in gender analysis. Her new book is entitled *Daughters of the Goddess, Daughters of Imperialism: African Women, Culture, Power and Democracy* (Zed Books, 2000).

Paul F. Knitter is professor of theology emeritus at Xavier University, Cincinnati. He received a licentiate in theology from the Pontifical Gregorian University in Rome (1966) and a doctorate from the University of Marburg, Germany (1972). Most of his research and publications have dealt with religious pluralism and interreligious dialogue. He is also general editor of Orbis Books' Faith Meets Faith series. Over the past fifteen years, Knitter has also been active in various peace groups working in El Salvador, especially Christians for Peace in El Salvador (CRISPAZ). He is also on the board of directors for the International Interreligious Peace Council.

David R. Loy is professor in the Faculty of International Studies at Bunkyo University, Chigasaki, Japan. His work is primarily in comparative philosophy and religion, particularly comparing Buddhist with modern Western thought. He is the author of *Nonduality: A Study in Comparative Philosophy* (1989); *Lack and Transcendence: The Problem of Death and Life in Psychotherapy, Existentialism and Buddhism* (1996), which was awarded the Frederick Streng Book Prize by the Society for Buddhist-Christian Studies; and *A Buddhist History of the West: Studies in Lack* (2001). A Zen student for many years, he is qualified as a sensei in the Sanbo Kyodan tradition.

Sallie McFague is Distinguished Theologian in Residence at the Vancouver School of Theology. For thirty years she taught at Vanderbilt Divinity School and retired in spring 2000. Her interests lie in the area of religious language and ecology, and she has published several books on this topic: *Models of God, The Body of God, Super, Natural Christians*, and the most recent one, *Life Abundant: Rethinking Theology and Economics for a Planet in Peril.*

Chandra Muzaffar, a Malaysian political scientist, was the first director of the Center for Civilizational Dialogue at the University of Malaya. Apart from writings on civilizational dialogue, he has also published extensively on religion, human rights, Malaysian politics, and international relations. His most recent book, co-authored with Sulak Sivaraksa, is entitled *Alternative Politics in Asia: A Buddhist-Muslim Dialogue*. Chandra Muzaffar is also the president of a Malaysian-based international nongovernmental organization, the International Movement for a Just World, which seeks to raise public consciousness on the moral and intellectual basis of global justice. He also sits on the boards of a number of other international NGOs concerned with social justice and civilizational dialogue.

Norman Solomon lives in Oxford, England, and has been a member of the faculties of theology and Oriental studies at Oxford University since 1995. He was born in Cardiff, South Wales, in 1933 and educated there and at the University of Cambridge. He has practiced as a rabbi in Orthodox congregations in England and, in 1983, founded the Centre for the Study of Judaism and Jewish-Christian Relations in Birmingham, England, which he directed until 1994. He is the author of several books, a keen musician, and has completed the London and New York marathons.

Zhou Qin received her Ph.D. in Chinese philosophy from Harvard University and is now teaching in the Department of Chinese Studies at the National University of Singapore. Her research interests include the religious traditions of early China, Confucian ethics in the classical period, and the Confucian tradition in modern transition. Among the books she has authored and co-authored are *On Contemporary Confucianism: From Xiong Shili to Mou Zongsan* and *Windows of Opportunity for Confucianism*. She has also published several articles on Confucian philosophy and other Chinese traditions. She is currently working in the area of Confucian ethics and the cosmological faith of the pre-Confucian era.

Index

Other Titles in the Faith Meets Faith Series

Toward a Universal Theology of Religion, Leonard Swidler, editor
The Myth of Christian Uniqueness, John Hick and Paul F. Knitter, editors
An Asian Theology of Liberation, Aloysius Pieris, S.J.
The Dialogical Imperative, David Lochhead
Love Meets Wisdom, Aloysius Pieris, S.J.
Many Paths, Eugene Hillman, C.S.Sp.
The Silence of God, Raimundo Panikkar
The Challenge of the Scriptures, Groupe de Recherches Islamo-Chrétien
The Meaning of Christ, John P. Keenan
Hindu-Christian Dialogue, Harold Coward, editor
The Emptying God, John B. Cobb, Jr., and Christopher Ives, editors
Christianity through Non-Christian Eyes, Paul J. Griffiths, editor
Christian Uniqueness Reconsidered, Gavin D'Costa, editor
Women Speaking, Women Listening, Maura O'Neill
Bursting the Bonds?, Leonard Swidler, Lewis John Eron, Gerard Sloyan, and Lester Dean, editors
One Christ—Many Religions, Stanley J. Samartha
The New Universalism, David J. Kreiger
Jesus Christ at the Encounter of World Religions, Jacques Dupuis, S.J.
After Patriarchy, Paula M. Cooey, William R. Eakin, and Jay B. McDaniel, editors
An Apology for Apologetics, Paul J. Griffiths
World Religions and Human Liberation, Dan Cohn-Sherbok, editor
Uniqueness, Gabriel Moran
Leave the Temple, Felix Wilfred, editor
The Buddha and the Christ, Leo D. Lefebure
The Divine Matrix, Joseph A. Bracken, S.J.
The Gospel of Mark: A Mahāyāna Reading, John P. Keenan
Revelation, History, and the Dialogue of Religions, David A. Carpenter

Salvations, S. Mark Heim
The Intercultural Challenge of Raimon Panikkar, Joseph Prabhu, editor
Fire and Water: Women, Society, and Spirituality in Buddhism and Christianity, Aloysius Pieris, S.J.
Piety and Power: Muslims and Christians in West Africa, Lamin Sanneh
Life after Death in World Religions, Harold Coward, editor
The Uniqueness of Jesus, Paul Mojzes and Leonard Swidler, editors
A Pilgrim in Chinese Culture, Judith A. Berling
West African Religious Traditions, Robert B. Fisher, S.V.D.
Hindu Wisdom for All God's Children, Francis X. Clooney, S.J.
Imagining the Sacred, Vernon Ruland, S.J.
Christian-Muslim Relations, Ovey N. Mohammed, S.J.
John Paul II and Interreligious Dialogue, Byron L. Sherwin and Harold Kasimow, editors
Transforming Christianity and the World, John B. Cobb, Jr.
The Divine Deli, John H. Berthrong
Experiencing Scripture in World Religions, Harold Coward, editor
The Meeting of Religions and the Trinity, Gavin D'Costa
Subverting Hatred: The Challenge of Nonviolence in Religious Traditions, Daniel L. Smith-Christopher, editor
Christianity and Buddhism: A Multi-Cultural History of their Dialogue, Whalen Lai and Michael von Brück
Islam, Christianity, and the West: A Troubled History, Rollin Armour, Sr.

About the Boston Research Center

The Boston Research Center for the 21st Century is an international peace institute founded in 1993 by Daisaku Ikeda, who is a Buddhist peace activist and president of Soka Gakkai International (SGI), a religious association with members in 181 countries.

The Center fosters dialogue among scholars and activists on common values across cultures and religions, seeking in this way to support an evolving global ethic for a peaceful twenty-first century. Currently, the focal points for the Center's work include the Earth Charter and youth, education for global citizenship, and women's leadership for peace.

Through public events, collaborations, and a variety of publications including a Web site (www.brc21.org), the Center creates opportunities for dialogue on global ethics, forums on women's leadership for peace, Global Citizen Awards, a newsletter, and books on common values. The Center's books provide curricular support for university courses in ethics, peace studies, comparative religion, and peace education.

Cover photo credits: Composite by John F. Levine based on an Image © Image 100/Royalty Free/Corbis and incorporating photos from Maryknoll Fathers & Brothers Image Resources Center by (clockwise from left) Robert T. McCahill/Bangladesh, Edward M. Gerlock/ Philippines, Jim Spillane/Guatemala, Sean Sprague/China, Joseph W. Towle/Bolivia, Eric Wheater/Peru.